CAMBRIDGE LIBRARY COLLECTION

Books of enduring scholarly value

Printing and Publishing History

The interface between authors and their readers is a fascinating subject in its own right, revealing a great deal about social attitudes, technological progress, aesthetic values, fashionable interests, political positions, economic constraints, and individual personalities. This part of the Cambridge Library Collection reissues classic studies in the area of printing and publishing history that shed light on developments in typography and book design, printing and binding, the rise and fall of publishing houses and periodicals, and the roles of authors and illustrators. It documents the ebb and flow of the book trade supplying a wide range of customers with products from almanacs to novels, bibles to erotica, and poetry to statistics.

An Inquiry into the Nature and Form of the Books of the Ancients

John Andrews Arnett was the pseudonym of John Hannett (1803–93), a printer and a pioneer in the study of modern and historical bookbinding methods. *An Inquiry into the Nature and Form of the Books of the Ancients* was published in 1837, following the success of *Bibliopegia*, his manual of bookbinding techniques. Having outlined the various ways in which written records were kept, and the development of the codex and of printing, Hannett devotes most of the book to the history of bookbinding. The book is well researched and illustrated, with many quotations from earlier works to support his clearly written narrative. Wills and accounts often describe books in terms of their binding, providing a way of following changing fashions in book coverings. He examines bindings from continental and oriental sources as well as English examples, before discussing modern binding practice and practitioners.

T0371330

Cambridge University Press has long been a pioneer in the reissuing of out-of-print titles from its own backlist, producing digital reprints of books that are still sought after by scholars and students but could not be reprinted economically using traditional technology. The Cambridge Library Collection extends this activity to a wider range of books which are still of importance to researchers and professionals, either for the source material they contain, or as landmarks in the history of their academic discipline.

Drawing from the world-renowned collections in the Cambridge University Library, and guided by the advice of experts in each subject area, Cambridge University Press is using state-of-the-art scanning machines in its own Printing House to capture the content of each book selected for inclusion. The files are processed to give a consistently clear, crisp image, and the books finished to the high quality standard for which the Press is recognised around the world. The latest print-on-demand technology ensures that the books will remain available indefinitely, and that orders for single or multiple copies can quickly be supplied.

The Cambridge Library Collection will bring back to life books of enduring scholarly value (including out-of-copyright works originally issued by other publishers) across a wide range of disciplines in the humanities and social sciences and in science and technology.

An Inquiry into the Nature and Form of the Books of the Ancients

With a History of the Art of Bookbinding, from the Times of the Greeks and Romans to the Present Day

JOHN HANNETT

CAMBRIDGE UNIVERSITY PRESS

Cambridge, New York, Melbourne, Madrid, Cape Town, Singapore,
São Paolo, Delhi, Dubai, Tokyo, Mexico City

Published in the United States of America by Cambridge University Press, New York

www.cambridge.org
Information on this title: www.cambridge.org/9781108024822

© in this compilation Cambridge University Press 2010

This edition first published 1837
This digitally printed version 2010

ISBN 978-1-108-02482-2 Paperback

See page 206.

ANCIENT BINDINGS.

AN INQUIRY

INTO THE

NATURE AND FORM

OF THE

BOOKS OF THE ANCIENTS;

WITH A

HISTORY

OF THE

ART OF BOOKBINDING,

FROM THE TIMES OF

THE GREEKS AND ROMANS TO THE PRESENT DAY;

INTERSPERSED WITH

BIBLIOGRAPHICAL REFERENCES TO MEN AND BOOKS

OF ALL AGES AND COUNTRIES.

ILLUSTRATED WITH NUMEROUS ENGRAVINGS.

BY JOHN ANDREWS ARNETT.

LONDON:
RICHARD GROOMBRIDGE.
EDINBURGH: OLIVER AND BOYD.—DUBLIN: CURRY AND CO.
PARIS: GALIGNANI.—NEW YORK: W. JACKSON.
1837.

London : G. H. Davidson, Printer, Tudor-street, Blackfriars' Bridge.

PREFACE.

THE following work aspires to the rank of a historical and chronological record of the art and science of composing books, and their subsequent embellishment,—a subject so intimately connected with literature, as to have ever been a matter of much speculation to the antiquarian and man of letters, as well as of great interest to the artist and general reader.

To the perusal of the works of Ames, Palmer, Stower, Hansard, and Johnson, on the History of Printing, may a desire to collect the dispersed records of the much older Art of Bookbinding, and to perpetuate the still existing specimens of the talent of early times (many fast hastening to, and all in progress of, decay), be said to have arisen, and the appearance of the present work be attributed. To effect this object, the slight notices of the form of books, and remarks on their embellishment, found in numerous publications devoted to bibliographical subjects, to the histories of countries, of a people, or of individuals, have been collected. These, as now arranged in chronological order, and embodied with a historical record and dissertations founded on personal inspection of many ancient bindings, will, it is presumed, be found to possess an interest and variety not hitherto attached to the subject.

Where an opportunity of consulting the works to which allusion has been found made by others, has not occurred, references have been given to the parties citing them ; but in all other cases the original authority. The references to the labours of such as have incidentally toiled in the same field will be found throughout scrupulously recorded ; as also to the productions of those, who, in a more extended manner, have devoted their time and talents to the subject. These are, the Rev. T. F. Dibdin, D.D., and the Rev. T. H. Horne, B.D. To the former gentleman, thanks are particularly tendered for the ready permission granted to copy some of the engravings, and make use of extracts from his valuable works. In the composition of the following pages, it has, on two occasions, been necessary more particularly to refer to them, viz. the *impressed*

---

calf bindings of the fifteenth century, and the *French bindings* of the same period. On this department of the History of Book-binding, the Doctor has been so diffuse, that little could be added. Such other specimens and remarks are therefore introduced, as were necessary to connect the style with the introduction of others; and various incidental matter relative to the characters of Grolier, De Thou, and the French Binders of their times; a preference being given to the Doctor's own statements, to any dishonest garbling or re-writing of this portion of the work.

To the Rev. T. H. Horne, thanks are also due for several valuable suggestions; and like acknowledgments to Sir S. R. Meyrick, the Very Rev. G. Gordon, Dean of Lincoln, the Rev. C. H. Hartshorne, the Rev. H. H. Baber, of the British Museum, the Rev. W. Cureton, of the Bodleian Library, Oxford, T. Thomson, Esq., of the Record Office, Edinburgh, J. B. Nichols, Esq., Mr. John Martin, Mr. John Bohn, and Mr. C. Knight, for hints, or assistance rendered in the pursuit of the following inquiries.

The illustrations for the early portion of the work, have been engraved principally from the "Antiquités d'Herculanum," by David. The others from sources named in the text, or from drawings made of existing bindings in the British Museum, &c., by Mr. James Lee, by whom nearly the whole of the engravings have been executed.

The work has been composed at intervals of leisure, from more serious occupations; and, if not embracing all the elegance of style by some desired, it is trusted will be found at all times clear and perspicuous. To this end, the object throughout has been to avoid all technicalities and vague speculations; to keep the truth of history and the value of utility constantly in view, without running into unnecessary diffuseness. The subject, it is presumed, will thus be found to address itself to every class of readers; and intimately connected as it is with literature, in all ages and countries, the frequent reference necessary to be made to the possessors of collections, and many scarce books existing in good preservation in public and private libraries, will, it is hoped, alike constitute an additional claim on the attention of the ANTIQUARIAN and BIBLIOGRAPHER.

April, 1837.

THE

BOOKS OF THE ANCIENTS,

&c.

CHAPTER I.

ON THE RECORDS AND WRITINGS OF THE EARLIEST
PEOPLE; THEIR FORM, AND METHOD OF PRESER-
VATION.

In the darkness of ages, the arts and sciences generally have been enveloped in obscurity :—of many,
not even the record of their existence, and of others,
merely the passing mention of their once general
prevalence, has been handed down to us   And
whilst those arts which must of necessity have first
occupied the thoughts and attention of mankind,
such as would contribute to their personal comfort,
to the supply of their wants, or to the defence of
their position and home, are scarcely known, we can
little expect that anything approaching to the refine-
ments of life, such as the records of their literature,
will be met with.   In the brief notices of the transactions of man soon after the creation, we find Jubal

referred to as the father of all such as handle the harp and organ, and Tubal-cain as an instructor of every artificer in brass and iron. To this may be added, the knowledge the earliest people possessed of the art of wine-making, of navigation and ship-building, as implied in the formation of the ark of Noah, of building and architecture, in the erection of the city and tower of Babel, of the making of arms for trained fighting-men, of images, of camels' furniture, and of chariots of war. And if we descend to the date assigned by Dr. Good[a] to the Book of Job, namely, 1200 years after the flood, it is certain that at that epoch metals were extracted from the earth and used for domestic purposes, for instruments of war, and for money; that various musical instruments were known, that written characters were in common use, that astronomy was cultivated as a science, and that mankind unquestionably were not living in the simple patriarchal state, since different ranks in society are in several instances familiarly mentioned; whilst it is at the same time quite evident, that the degree of intellectual acquirement and of refinement which would allow of the composition of the work itself, could not have been low in the scale of human cultivation.[b] Considering these facts, and reasoning from the general improvement of society in all ages, where men have

[a] Good's Book of Job, p. 46.——[b] Beke's Origines Biblicæ, vol. i. p. 52.

congregated together, it may be pronounced all but
certain, that some degree of refinement, and a regard
for learning, had been arrived at by the antediluvian
world, particularly so when the general belief of the
Mosaic account gives a period of 2000 years duration
to the earth prior to the deluge.

Of the mode adopted in the earliest times to
transmit to after generations the records of the preceding ones, an impenetrable darkness hangs around ;
and in attempting any description, conjecture alone
can be the foundation. And if this uncertainty as to
the very existence of their records is the case, how
much more difficult becomes the path by which we
can draw any conclusion as to the material of which
they were composed, or of the manner of preserving
them. That the antediluvians did arrive at a considerable degree of proficiency in many of the arts,
has been shown, and we may fairly conclude that
some method had been invented, by which the
thoughts and opinions of the learned might be com-
municated in some more durable manner than oral
testimony. But nothing exists to prove this to be
so ; we, therefore, are left to draw the inference, from
what has been transmitted relative to later times,
that a similar mode had been adopted, and progression made, in periods anterior to them. Taking this
as our guide, and allowing that there is much on the
subject we must be content to remain ignorant of,
it will be necessary to ascertain what has reached us
relative to the materials on, and form in, which

the early inhabitants of the earth inscribed their records.

Engraving, or sculpture on stone, appears to have been the first method of writing; the great and noble actions of nations and men were cut on entire rocks and mountains.[c] This custom was continued for many ages, and remains still exist in Denmark, Norway, the deserts of Tartary, and Judea. The absence of rocks in many situations, or for the better keeping before the eye of youth the acts and deeds of their forefathers, doubtless suggested the pillar or column. Josephus makes mention of two, one of stone, the other of brick, on which the children of Seth wrote their inventions and astronomical discoveries.[d] Porphyri also speaks of some stone pillars in Crete, on which the ceremonies of the Corybantes in their sacrifices were recorded[e] Many of the obelisks brought from Egypt are of this character, and there are some ancient monuments of the same kind of writing remaining in that country, more particularly among the ruins of Persepolis.[f] These inscriptions commemorated events in history and discoveries in science, and to them the ancient historians, Sanchoniatho and Herodotus, acknowledge their obligations.[g] Mr. Drummond, however, is of opinion that the first essays in the art of writing

[c] Job xix. v. 24.——[d] Antiquities of the Jews, book i. c. 2.——[e] Warton's English Poetry, vol. i. p. xxvii. &c.——Maurice s Babylon, p. 186.——[g] Herculanensia;—Hon. W. Drummond, p. 98.

must have been on softer materials than stones.
Whether so or not, it is certain that the time and
labour necessary to carve on stone, would soon lead
men to consider of some more expeditious mode of
recording their thoughts and discoveries ; as well as
to multiply their number. We find clay was early
used for the purpose, and stamps made by which it
was impressed, and then submitted to the action of
the sun or fire to harden. To this class the Baby-
lonian bricks belong, the inscriptions on which
doubtless were intended for the propagation of
science, to the inculcation of some special facts, or
the record of some useful memorial. And though
the meaning of these inscriptions is unknown, the
preservation of some of the bricks through a period
of some thousand years, proves that the ancients
rightly calculated on the mode they adopted in
perpetuating their discoveries. These bricks were
employed in the building of their public edifices.
From them further advances were made, which ultimately led to the formation of books. This progress
is shown in the following sketch of a burnt clay pillar,
of about the same period as those before referred to.
It also displays a considerable improvement in the
formation of the characters. This pillar, with severa
of the bricks, are preserved in the library of Trinity
College, Cambridge.

h Fosbroke's Cyclop. of Antiquities, vol. i. p. 235.
i Hansard's Typographia, p. 2.

Mr. Hansard, who minutely examined this pillar,
considered it a rare piece of ancient learning and art,
and a work of great public importance at the time it
was executed.   He says: "One of these printed
pieces might contain a complete subject; or a subject might occupy several of them, which altogether
formed a series; each piece answering, as it were,
such a purpose as the leaf of a book; one following
another in regular order, from the beginning to the
end of any subject, as the sheets in a volume.   From

a succession of these printed miniature monuments might numerous sets be made; and thus might laws, astronomical observations, historical annals, and any other subject of interest to mankind, be recorded."[k]

This opinion, there can be little doubt, is a right conclusion. And to confirm it we find, even long after the acknowledged period of the invention of letters, that engraving on similar pillars of stone and other durable substances was still adopted. Pollux and Suidas state that the pieces of brass on which the public documents in their time were written, were of a cubical form.[l]

The first books, then, if we may so call them, were simply in the form of pillars or tables, of which frequent mention is made in Scripture under the name of *Sephir*. When, however, the ancients had matters a little longer to treat of, they would adopt materials more suited to their purpose. Hence, wood, slate, horn, plates of lead and copper, leaves of trees, and other materials, according to the local circumstances of different nations, and their progress in the arts, were used to write such things upon as hey were desirous to have transmitted to posterity.'[m]

That a ready mode of writing was in general use, or at least well understood by the learned, previous to the delivery of the tables of the law, is proved by the command given to Moses, " Write this for a me-

[k] Typographia, p. 10.——[l] Herculanensia, p. 104.——
[m] Fosbroke's Ency. of Antiquities, vol. i 235.

morial in a *book*." It is observable, that there is not
the least hint to induce us to believe that writing was
then newly invented: on the contrary, we may conclude, that Moses understood what was meant by
writing in a book; otherwise God would have in-
structed him, as he had done Noah in building the
ark ; for he would not have been commanded to *write*
in a *book,* if he had been *ignorant of the art of writing:*
but Moses expressed no difficulty of comprehension,
when he received this command.[n]   He may have
become acquainted with the art of writing in Egypt,
which country, we learn from the Old Testament,
was long previously acquainted with all those arts of
civilization and government, and notions of property,
which usually belong to nations which have been long
settled and civilized.[o]

Slight as are the notices of the writings of the early
ages of the world, little can here be stated relative to
ancient bookbinding, but that some mode of preservation of documents which must have required so
much care to execute, was early devised, cannot be
doubted; and therefore the art may be dated as
almost coeval with the science of composing books :
and that both one and the other would soon follow
the invention of hieroglyphic characters and letters,
though it must be after the latter period to which we
must look for anything that can decidedly be called

[n] Astle's Origin and Progress of Writing, pp. 12, 13. ——
[o] Sharpe's Early History of Egypt, p. 4.

bookbinding. Previous to this, the preservation of their tables, &c., was by means of cases of wood, stone, or earthenware, of which we have an example in the commandments given to Moses. But that writings in his time were of some extent, is shown in the book of Exodus (xxiv. 4—7), where we find that Moses *wrote* all the *words* and all the judgments of the Lord, contained in the twenty-first and two following chapters. What was the material, or what the form of the original book of the law, cannot be ascertained. Montfauçon believed it was written on skins ; and considering that the roll is the form still adopted in all the synagogues of the Jews, we shall not be hazarding too much to state it to have been so since its first promulgation by Moses to the people. Some progress must have been made before this ; and at whatever period books were first formed, a necessity would arise of uniting the several parts together, for the more ready reference, as well as their better preservation. This, however slight or rudely performed, was the foundation of an art, which in our day has arrived at a style of decoration scarcely to be surpassed by any other.

That the writers of the books would be the first binders, it is fair to presume ; from which class, perhaps, or from others trained to the art, would proceed a race of artisans restricted to this branch alone. But there is again no data to establish the fact, and we can only hazard the conjecture, seeing that the details of all the arts for many ages are alike unknown.

This may be attributable to the circumstances of the times, or to the habits of the nations of antiquity. The Chaldeans, Phœnicians, Syrians, and Egyptians, all bordering upon each other, were alike early versed in the arts of life. From all that is known of the latter, either from Greek authors or from modern discoveries in the antiquities of Egypt, they appear to have been a nation of practised manipulators, mechanics, and workmen. The distribution of the people into ranks, and particular occupations to the same families from generation to generation, confined the knowledge possessed by each class, and never contributed to form a common stock of information. Hence the political system of the country provided for a succession of hereditary artists; and when that system was destroyed by the conquest of Egypt, the *peculiar* arts of the Egyptians were entirely lost.[p]

But the remains of their greatness, and evidences of their ability, were an example to their conquerors. The Greeks have abundantly borne testimony to how much the world is indebted to the Egyptians for architecture, geometry, agriculture, irrigation, letters, and paper. To some of these we shall more particularly allude in the next chapter.

[p] Brayley's Utility of the Knowledge of Nature, p. 57—59.

CHAPTER II.

BOOKS FROM THEIR FIRST KNOWN FORM, AND BOOK-
BINDING IN THE TIMES OF THE GREEKS AND
ROMANS.

A RAY of light now beams on our subject, for
though time, and the ravages of war, have swept
away, with few exceptions, all the original written
documents, records, and literature of the once powerful and learned nations of the earth, still we are now
enabled, by the notices met with in ancient writers,
to speak with certainty of the materials on which the
first known books were written and the form in
which they were made up, as well as of the covering
adopted for their greater security.

The first books were square, and consisted of but
one leaf, or tablet. These were composed of wood,
&c., as before stated. The etymology of the word
book, and its equivalent in many languages, indicates
that they were originally written on vegetable substances. Thus, from the Greek *biblos,* the Latin
liber, codex, folium, and *tabula,* we learn that books
were sometimes inscribed on the inner bark and

sometimes on boards cut off the main body of the tree; and the English word *book*, derived from the Saxon *boc*, the root of which is the northern *beuch*, a beach or service tree, evidently shows that the books of our ancestors were of a similar fabric. Thus we find that the leaves of the palm tree,[a] and the finest and thinnest part of the bark of such trees as the tilia, the philyra, a species of linden, the lime, the ash, the maple, and the elm, were first used when men began to extend their writings and disquisitions.[b] This custom existed in the time of Ulpian, who mentions it, and even still continues in nations where little progress has been made in refinement, copies of books being frequently brought to this country from the east, written on oblong slips of bark or reed, fastened together by strings at each end. In Ceylon they still write on the leaves of the talipot: and the Bramin MSS. in the Talinga language, sent to England from Fort St. George, are written on leaves of the Ampana, or *Palma Malabarica*.[c] Numbers of these books, executed in a fine and beautiful character, and bound together with boards, may be seen in the library of the East India Company. A very curious library of this description was discovered some time ago among the Calmuc Tartars, by the Russians. The books were exceedingly long and narrow, the leaves very thick and made of bark of trees, smeared over with a double

[a] Pliny, l. xiii. 10.——[b] Astle's Writing, p 201.——[c] Horne's Bibliography, vol. i. p. 42.

varnish; the ink or writing being white on a black ground.[d]

The early writers successively made use of linen and cotton cloths; of the skins, intestines, and even shoulder blades, of various animals; of table books of wax, ivory, and lead; of the skins of fishes; and of the intestines of serpents. To some of these we shall have again to refer, in the course of our researches. These substances, in those countries where knowledge and letters had made some progress, soon fell into disuse on the introduction of the Egyptian papyrus, which unquestionably is the earliest of any of the various kinds of paper with which the ancients were acquainted. It was in very common use in the time of Alexander, but the exact date of its discovery is unknown; and even where it was first made is matter of dispute; but it is very evident from the ancient papyri found at Thebes and elsewhere, and from Isaiah xix. 7, that it was used for writing long before the period above referred to. According to Isidore, it was first made at Memphis; and according to others, in Seide, or Upper Egypt. It was manufactured from the inner films of the papyrus, or biblos, a sort of flag or bulrush, growing in the marshes of Egypt. The outer skin being taken off, the films or inner skins were separated from the stalk, laid on a table, moistened with the glutinous waters of the Nile, and afterwards

[d] Hist. de Academy, R. Inscriptions, tom. iii. p. 6.

c

pressed together, and dried in the sun.[e] Bruce, the African traveller, who made some experiments on the subject, however, denies this property of the waters of the Nile.

Successive experiments in the manufacture of skins ultimately led to the invention of vellum or parchment. This discovery is attributed to the prohibition of the exportation of the papyrus from Egypt, by one of the Ptolemies; in order to throw an obstacle in the way of Eumenes, king of Pergamus, who endeavoured to rival him in the magnificence of his library. Thus left without material, we find from Vossius that Eumenes invented a method of cleaning skins on both sides, before only written on one. It was called *Charta Pergamena* from the name of the capital. Parchment or vellum was also used in Egypt. Pliny says—

" Mox æmulatione circa bibliothecas regum," &c.

The same is related by Œlian and Hieronymus with little variation. The Saracens had beautiful parchment, equal in appearance to paper.

Having thus shown the nature of the materials of which the ancients composed their books, and which, in the infancy of the art, is so intimately connected with bookbinding as to form a part of the subject, we shall now proceed to the consideration of the form first adopted, the mode of preservation, and the

[e] Townley's Illustrats. of Bib. Lit. i. 45.——[f] Bayle, Chalmers, &c.——[g] Herculanensia, p. 106.——[h] Gibbon's Rome, ix. 51.

style of ornament in use in early times. The first
form, when more flexible materials began to be
used, was the roll, called by the Romans, *volu-
mina* and also *scapi*.[i] This, doubtless, was the
most ancient mode of binding, and at first consisted in sewing the different sheets or leaves
together, till the volume or book was finished.
Only one book was included in a volume, so that a
work generally consisted of as many volumes as
books. They might measure, when extended, one
yard and a half wide, and fifty long.   They were
written in separate pages, and fastened parallel to
each other, so that the reader perused one page,
then rolled it up at one end, unrolling the next page
and so on to the end, as is seen in the following
engraving from a painting found at Pompeii.

[i] Ency. Methodique.——[k] Fabricius' Bibl. Antiq. c.xix. p. 607.

Of the great and early skill in making these rolls, an instance is found in Josephus, in reference to a copy of the law, sent to Ptolemy Philadelphus, which was written in letters of gold, upon skins so artfully put together, that the joinings did not appear. The most extraordinary papyrus that perhaps exists in any collection, is a funeral roll discovered at Memphis, and now in the British Museum. It is considered to be about *three thousand* years old, and appears to relate to a scribe of high rank named *Nebsenai*, of the temple of *Pthah Sokar*. When entirely opened, it is considered this roll will measure one hundred feet in length.

The GREEKS derived their first knowledge of the *roll* from the EGYPTIANS, and the style passed for a long series of years under the name of *Egyptian binding*. This continued the general form for many ages, the libraries of the Greeks and Romans consisting of rolls for some centuries after the Christian era. And it will now be seen that the whole arcana of the manufacture and binding of books was well understood by these once powerful people.

The writings of the Greeks do not furnish any detail as to the mode of binding books, but that they were fully alive to the importance of the subject, may be inferred from the circumstance of the Athenians erecting a statue to the memory of *Phillatius*, the discoverer of a substance to make the pages or

---

[m] Antiq. of Jews, book xii. p. 405.

sheets adhere together.[n] But the writers among the
Romans, who doubtless obtained much of their
knowledge from the Greeks, enter into the minutia
of the art, and thus furnish us with every thing
necessary for a full description of the form and mode
of preservation of the records of early times. The
Romans had their *librarii, librarioli, bibliopegi,* and
bibliopola ; answering to our *printer, engraver, binder,*
and *bookseller.* The *librarii* multiplied books by
transcribing MSS. ; the *librarioli* illustrated them by
ornament on the title-pages, margins, and termina-
tions ;—the *bibliopegi* employed their skill on the embellishment of their exteriors :—and the *bibliopola*
were engaged in the disposal of them.

It is with the *bibliopegus* that we have more particularly to interest ourselves in this treatise, and of
his functions we shall, in the general description of
ancient bindings, have constantly to speak. The
duties of the other branches employed in the production of books will be introduced in illustration of
various references it will be necessary to make relative to the form of ancient records.

In the infancy of the art, the sheets or pages, it
has been stated, were fastened, or sewn together by
strings. The damage caused by this proceeding,
where the material was so frail as the papyrus, led to
the invention of paste or glue by an Athenian,
whose countrymen, Olympiodorus states, accorded

---

[u] Noveau Traite de Diplom, tom. iii. p. 60.

to him the honour before referred to. Of its use for this purpose, Cicero, in a letter to his friend Atticus, has left a proof,[o] and Pliny confirms it. Pollux also mentions writers and vendors of books, and the glutination of them.[p]

When the sheets intended to form one volume or book, were thus attached together, another, generally of parchment, was in like manner fastened to the left margin of the first page, for the purpose of forming the cover, and another at the termination. The interior of the first was reserved for the dedicatory epistle, and which, from its being found on the opening of the roll, *a limine*, was called *liminaire*. After the embellishment of the work by the skill of the *librariolus*, it then passed into the hands of the *bibliopegus*.

The first operation of the Greek and Roman bookbinder was to cut the margins above and below perfectly even, and the sheets at beginning and end square. He then gave the exterior the most perfect polish possible by means of the pumice-stone, with which substance the writers had previously smoothed the interior. Horace, Pliny, Martial, Ovid, and Catullus all bear testimony to this use of the pumice, and to the present day it is adopted by bookbinders in some of their operations.

The cover, which was called the *involucrum*, was then fastened to a cylinder of wood, round which the volume was rolled. Porphyrio states they sometimes were formed of bone, and sometimes even of

gold.[q] They had frequently one of these rollers at
each extremity.   At the ends of the cylinder a ball
or knob was then affixed, which was employed as a
handle for evolving the scroll, it being at one time a
reputed crime to take hold of the roll itself.   The
outside of the volume was called *frons*, the balls at
the end *umbilici*, or, according to Ovid and Tibullus,
cornua.   These were generally made of bone, wood,
or horn, and often carved and adorned with ivory,
silver, gold, or precious stones.   The value or importance of the manuscript was sometimes indicated
by the style of ornament introduced upon these bosses,
and many of them, without doubt, were inscribed
in the centre or round the edge with the name of the
author of the work.   It appears, however, from the
papyri found at Herculaneum, that this expensive
style of embellishment was not general, but that
many of their writings were simply rolled up, with a
ticket or label attached to the centre, bearing the
title of the work, as shown in the following engraving
of some of the rolls discovered there.

q Dibdin's Bib. Decameron, vol. ii. p. 480.
r Fabric. Bibl. Antiq. c. xix, p. 607.

This illustration also gives a further idea of the form of ancient books.

The cover, which, according to Achilles Statius, was at first woven of the fibrous bark of some tree, was embellished by the addition of colour and ornament. Purple and scarlet were the most general. Martial says

> " Sunt quoque mutatæ ter quinque volumina formæ,
>   Purpureo fulgens habitu, radiantibus uncis ;"

and speaking of a *libraria* opposite the *Forum Julii,* "There you may buy Martial, polished with pumice-stone, and ornamented with purple, for five denarii."[*] But in another epigram he enters into the details of the binding of a book in his time—

> " Festina tibi vindicem parare,
>   Ne nigram cito raptus in culinam
>   Cordyllas madida tegas papyro,
>   Vel thuris, piperisque sis cucullus.
>   Faustini fugis in sinum ? Sapisti.
>   Cedro nunc licet ambules perunctus,
>   Et frontis gemino decens honore
>   Pictis luxurieris umbilicis ;
>   Et te purpura delicata velet,
>   Et cocco rubeat superbus index." [t]

We see herein that the patronage of literary efforts was then considered of some value, and that the work of the poet was about to appear under that of *Faustinus*. The leaf perfumed with oil of cedar, and decorated with a double ornament, the painted bosses, the bright purple cover, and the magnificent title in red letters, gives an idea of the splendour of the

Epigram i. 118.——[t] Epigram ii. book 2.

whole appearance. To this notice of what Martial wished to be performed on his work, another proof of the elegance of some of the Roman books is found in the directions given by Ovid relative to the omission of all ornament. The poet in exile, sent his book to Rome, and directed that it should be presented in a simple manner, typical of grief and affliction, " in the costume of an exile."

> " Nec te purpureo velent vaccinia fuco :
> Non est conveniens luctibus ille color.
> Nec titulus minio, nec cedro charta notetur:
> Candida nec nigra cornua fronte geras.
> Felices ornent hæc instrumenta libellos :
> Fortunæ memorem te decet esse meæ.
> Nec fragili geminæ poliantur pumice frontes :
> Hirsutus passis ut videare comis." [v]

Let not, he says, violets adorn it with their purple dye,[*] that colour is not suitable to grief, nor let the title be ornamented with vermillion, nor the leaf with cedar. He wishes no exterior embellishment to appear, and the polish of the pumice to be omitted, so that the roughness and remnants of hair remaining on the parchment might convey the idea of his own, through his affliction, "that it may appear rough with dishevelled hair."

Horace[w] and Tibullus[x] confirm all that has been advanced above on the practice of the art among the Romans, and many other passages in Martial might

---

[v] Ovid de Tristibus, Eleg. ad Librum, 1.——[w] Epistle xx. 1.
——[x] Book iii. eleg. 1.

[*] Servius says that *vaccinia* were violets of a purple colour.—Pliny that it was a shrub in Gaul adapted for dyeing.

be quoted to the same effect. Tibullus appears to refer to a cover coloured with yellow :—

"Lutea sed niveum involvat membrana libellum ;"

but it may be a question whether the colour of the parchment, of which the cover was formed, and which assumes a yellow appearance from age, is not the right construction of the passage.

To Catullus we are indebted for a minute and elaborate description of ancient binding. In the dedication to Cornelius Nepos he writes—

"With pumice dry, just polished fine,
To whom present this book of mine,
This little volume, smart and new." x

And in another of his poems, in ridicule of a person named Suffenus, he gives us what may be considered a complete description of the best binding in the time of Cicero :—

"AD VARRUM.

"Suffenus iste, Varre, quem probe nosti,
Homo est venustus, et dicax, et urbanus ;
Idemque longe plurimos facit versus.
Puto esse ego illi millia aut decem aut plura.
Perscripta, nec sic, ut fit, in palimpsesto
Relata ; chartæ regiæ, novi libri,
Novi umbilici, lora rubra, membrana
Directa plumbo, et pumice omnia æquata." y

which has been thus rendered :—

"Suffenus, that wretch, whom my Varus well knows,
So pretty, so prating, so over polite,
Has a genius for verse that incessantly flows,
Has a muse which ten thousand fine things can indite.

x Catullus, English Translation, 2 vols. 8vo.——y Ode 22.

His paper is royal, not common, or bad;
His wrappers, his bosses, are totally new;
His sheets smooth'd by pumice, are all ruled with lead,
And bound with a riband of rose-coloured hue." [2]

The reference to the covers and bosses being of a new character, shows that the custom was to introduce great variety in the style of ornament. The *directa plumbo*, M. Peignot, in his Essay on the Books of the Ancients, thinks refers to the parchment of which the cover was composed, being cut with a square, from Catullus appearing to direct attention to the exterior form and condition of the binding; and further grounds his opinion from the book or roll being described as written on *chartæ regiæ*, and the covers being of parchment, *membrana*, as above described.

The *lora rubra* of Catullus were two strings of coloured riband or leather, attached to the last sheet or cover of the volume, round which, when it was rolled up, they were fastened so as to keep the whole tight and firm, and prevent the introduction of dust and insects.

On the outside of the cover the title of the work was generally inscribed. Chrysostom, who flourished in the fourth century, and who, doubtless, founded his argument on what he had frequently seen done at Constantinople, or by the more eastern princes who had business to transact with the Greek emperors, very particularly alludes to this custom. In his re-

English Translation.

marks on a disputed passage of the Bible, he observes that it referred to the title written on the
wrapper, which signified "The Messiah cometh."
And Aquilla, who flourished one hundred years
earlier, gives the same interpretation.[a] This suggests
a more distinct idea of the passage; as when referred
to the case in which the roll was enclosed, the impression becomes clear and energetic, implying that
the subject of the book is that " the Messiah cometh,"
which title might with great propriety be wrote or
embroidered on the wrapper or case in which it was
kept.[b]

The title consisted of a square piece of fine vellum
or parchment, glued on the cover in such manner
that, when rolled up, it appeared near the top, something similar to the titles of the books of the present
day. For this purpose the finest description was
selected. Cicero begs his friend to send him two of
his workmen, and wishes them to bring some fine
parchment, for making the titles of the books.[c] These
title pieces were generally of a darker colour than the
cover, and the letters formed of gold.

Recent discoveries have confirmed these views.
The collection of James Burton, Esq., formed during
his travels in Egypt, contained some specimens of
papyrus rolls, discovered in the tombs at Thebes,
which fully illustrates the subject, and also prove a

<hr />

[a] Calmet's Dictionary, vol. iii. p. 129, ed. 1836.——[b] Har-
mer's Observations on Scripture, vol. iv. p. 10.——[c] Letters
to Atticus, iv. 4.

considerable advance in the art by the Egyptians. One, in the hieroglyphic character, is inclosed in a curiously worked piece of leather, and has been covered with gold.   Another contains a short incription on the outside, and a third, now in the British Museum, a long one on the cover.

These specimens also show that the ancients were well acquainted with the process of gilding on leather and other substances, and that they so embellished the covers of their books is now placed beyond question.   It is evident the art of impression was well understood, as we find from the Scriptures that seals and coins were in use from the earliest periods, as well as brands and other instruments for the purpose of marking.   Virgil makes mention of brands with letters being used in his time for marking cattle, &c. with the owner's name.   The various seals, found in the tombs, and brought from Egypt in our day, as well as the certainty of many of their ornamental decorations being formed by pressure, abundantly confirms all that ancient writers have recorded.

The engraving gives the general appearance of the roll when completed.

D

From the perishable nature of the material of which the rolls and their coverings were composed, and the destruction of them in the war and strife of nations, it is seen that very few perfect specimens have been preserved to our times. The excavations at Herculaneum, the discovery of the ruins of which took place in 1713, has thrown some further light upon the subject. Here, after a lapse of nearly two thousand years, 1756 papyri have been acquired. Thirty-nine years after its first discovery, in making an excavation in a garden at Resina, in the remains of a house supposed to have belonged to L. Piso, were found a great number of papyrus rolls. They were ranged in presses round the sides of a small room, in the centre of which was a sort of rectangular book-case ; many of the rolls were at first destroyed by the workmen, who, from the colour given by age, took them to be sticks of charcoal. When, however, it was discovered that they were ancient manuscripts, the attention of the learned was directed towards their preservation. Father Piaggi invented a machine which is still employed for unrolling them, but many of them have been destroyed,—some crumbling into dust on the slightest touch. His late majesty, George IV., then prince of Wales, took much interest in the matter, and at his own private cost employed several gentlemen in the task of unrolling and decyphering them.[d] Among others, Sir H. Davy visited the spot for the

[d] Herculanensia, preface i.

purpose of assisting, but from some supposed impedi-
ments which obstructed his research, gave up the
experiment, after a little success had attended his
endeavours. It is to the shape of these rolls, and the
coverings they may have had, we have to refer: in
shape, the engraving at page 19 gives a correct representation, and of the state in which they were
found, two letters received in this country, about the
middle of the last century, present a full account.
One, from Camillo Paderni, keeper of the museum at
Portici, among other things, describes a room, the
floor of which was formed of mosaic work. He says,
" it appears to have been a library, adorned with
presses, inlaid with different sorts of wood, disposed
in rows, at the top of which were cornices." He
was buried in that spot more than ten days; he took
away three hundred and twenty-seven manuscripts,
all in Greek characters; there was also a bundle,
consisting of eighteen volumes, *wrapped round with
bark of tree;* they were Latin. The second, from
another person, describes a chamber of a house in
Herculaneum, where was found a great quantity of
rolls, about half a palm long, and round; they appeared like roots of wood, all black, and seeming to
be only of one piece; one of them falling on the
ground, it broke in the middle, and many letters were
observed, by which it was first known that the rolls
were of papyrus. There were about one hundred
and fifty rolls in wooden cases, much burnt. This
writer mentions the unrolling of a tract on music, by

Philodemus, which had about sixty columns, each column having twenty lines, of the third of a palm long. He also says there were Latin manuscripts, some of which were so voluminous, that, unrolled, they would take up a hundred palms.[e] A long interval took place between the publication of this treatise and any subsequent fragments, and even up to the present time little further progress has been made,[f]

In addition to the care and attention bestowed on the preparation and execution of these rolls by the ancients, they were not less mindful of their preservation. They employed a species of oil extracted from the cedar tree, to prevent their destruction from moths, worms, and other liable injuries.[g] Pliny says that the books of Numa were preserved under ground for five hundred and thirty-five years, from having been rubbed with *cedrium*, and enclosed in boxes formed of cedar.[h] The testimony of Ovid, Catullus, and others, has been before adduced as to its application for this purpose.

In addition to the coverings of the rolls, the ancients were accustomed to further protect them from injury by placing the most valuable in cases or chests of cedar wood, with the titles or labels at top in the following manner.

---

[e] Herculanensia, 192.——[f] Edinburgh Review. xlviii. 353—and Quarterly Review, v. 1.——[g] Vitruvius, ii. 11.——[h] Hist. Natura, xiii. 13.

This case was called by them *scrinium*, and *capsa*, or *capsula*, and was generally of a circular form, from its readier adaptation to the shape of the rolls. The ancients, in times of war, devastation, and rapacity, buried their writings in the earth, and this may at first have given rise to the *scrinium*. We have an instance of this in the twenty-second of Jeremiah, where he ordered the writings which he delivered to Baruch to be put in an earthen vessel. Whatever it may have been originally, it became afterwards a general sort of *bookcase*. Catullus, in excuse to Manlius for not sending him some verses, pleads having only one box of his books with him. This also proves that they were in the habit of taking a number of books with them to whatever place business or pleasure might lead, forming a sort of travelling library, as one of these boxes would contain several volumes. Some of them were highly ornamented. One found at Herculaneum, but which crumbled to dust soon after its discovery, bore busts of Demosthenes, Epicurus, Hermes, and Zeno.

While the roll was the form adopted for the lengthened works of the ancients, they appear for a long period to have made use of table books or *pugillaria*, for the purposes of taking notes, keeping accounts, &c. These were tablets of ivory, wood, or metal, thinly covered with wax, the writing upon which, with a stylus or iron pen, could be erased and written in again at pleasure.[i] Pliny[j] states that the public acts, among the most remote nations were written in leaden books. The existence of books formed of this metal is further supported by the testimony of Job, Suetonius, and Frontinus. The eminent antiquarian, Montfaucon, purchased a book at Rome in the year 1799, which he describes as composed entirely of lead :—" It is about four inches long by three wide. Not only the pieces which form the cover, but also all the leaves, in number six, the stick inserted into the rings, which hold the leaves together, the hinges and the nails, are all of lead, without exception."[k] It contained Egyptian gnostic figures, and writing. Montfaucon presented it to M. the Cardinal de Bouillon, but what has become of it is unknown. These leaden plates were frequently so extremely thin that they might easily be rolled up. Œneas Philiorceticus tells us that they were beaten with a hammer

[i] Note to Catullus, Ode 39.——[j] Nat. Hist. xiii. c. 1.——
[k] Moutfaucon, Antiq. Expliq. ii. 378.

until they were rendered very thin and pliable.[1]
Catullus[m] adverts to some wanton girl, who had
jestingly stolen his pugillaria or poetical notes. One
of these from Herculaneum is here represented.

They were connected together at the back by rings,
and consisted of from two to six or eight leaves,
having in the centre of each a slight projection or
button, to prevent the notes on the wax being destroyed or defaced. According to the number of the
leaves, they were called duplices, triplices, quintu-
plices, &c. The duplice has been introduced above,
and from the same source we are enabled to present
the triplice.

[1] Herculanensia, 100.——[m] Ode 39.

They were in use in the time of Homer, and accord-
to Pliny were introduced before the Trojan war.

> " The dreadful token of his dire intent,
> He in the *gilded tables* wrote and sent." [o]

Martial[p] makes mention of tablets of parchment
covered with wax.

The convenience of the square form in these tablets
ultimately led to its adoption for almost every description of writing.   The honour of the introduction
of binding, composed of separate leaves, as now universally practised throughout Europe, has been accorded to Eumenes, king of Pergamus, the same to
whom we have before referred as the inventor of
parchment. [q]

When the folded form came into use, the necessity
of a cover would become more apparent than for the
rolls, and hence gradually arose bookbinding in its
present shape.—At first the leaves were simply tied
together with riband, the riband forming a hinge
similar to the rings in the tablets before represented.
The form and manner will be understood by the following engraving.

[n] Herculanensia, 101.——[o] Homer's Iliad, vi. 168. ——
[p] xiv. ep. 7.——[q] Vossius, Bayle, Montfaucon, &c.

The cover at first, no doubt, would be a simple leaf of parchment, or some other skin. This would soon be found of itself insufficient, and probably suggest the use of boards, which were very early adopted. Bruce, the Abyssinian traveller, had in his possession a large and very perfect manuscript on papyrus; "a gnostic book, full of their dreams," which had been dug up at Thebes, and which he believed was the only perfect one then known. Speaking of it, he says, "the boards or covers for binding the leaves, are of papyrus root, covered first with the coarse pieces of the paper, and then with leather, in the same manner as it would be done now. It is a book that we should call a small folio, and I apprehend that the shape of the book, where papyrus is employed, was always of the same form with those of the moderns." In this latter remark Bruce is decidedly wrong. "The woody part of the root of the papyrus served for boards or coverings of the leaves. We know that this was anciently one use of it, both from Alcæus and Anacreon. The Ethiopians use wood for the outer covering of their books, and cover them with leather." ʳ

A more recent traveller, Dr. Hogg, has added to our store of knowledge on the early form of books, in a description of two papyri found at Thebes. He relates that "among the various objects of antiquity which were purchased from the Arabs, at Thebes,

Travels, vii. 8.

were two papyri, the one in Coptic, the other in
Greek ; both in the form of books. The Greek papyrus has been discovered to contain a portion of the
Psalms. The leaves, of about ten inches in length,
by seven in width, are arranged, and have been sewn
together like those of an ordinary book. They are
formed of strips of the papyrus plant, crossing each
other at right angles. They were both discovered
among the rubbish of an ancient convent at Thebes,
remarkable as still presenting some fragments of an
inscription, purporting to be a pastoral letter from
Athanasius, patriarch of Alexandria, who died A.D.
371.* The portion of the Psalms is now in the
British Museum, and consists of about thirty leaves.
The Coptic MS. contains one hundred and fifty
pages, folded in the form now adopted by us, but has
never been bound. It was in the collection of J.
Burton, Esq., lately sold by Messrs. Sotheby and
Son. Mr. Thorp, the bookseller, of Piccadilly, was
the purchaser, at the sum of 84*l.*

These discoveries prove a very early knowledge of,
and considerable proficiency in the art as now practised. When once the leaves were secured, the subsequent stages of covering and ornamenting would
soon follow. Bruce describes the book he had as
being covered with leather, and Suidas, who lived in
the tenth century, and who would reason from
personal knowledge of bindings of much earlier

* Visit to Alexandria, &c. ii. p. 312.

times, however erroneous his opinions on alchemy may have been, confirms the use of leather for the purpose of binding by the ancients. In his Lexicon, he describes chemistry as the art of making gold, and states that the *golden fleece*, in search of which Jason and the Argonauts went, was nothing else than a book *bound in sheep skin*, which taught the art of making gold.

The materials used and style of decoration adopted by the ancients for the embellishment of their rolls, has been described. All this knowledge would, when a more ample field for display, which the square form presented, arose, be brought into requisition, and considerably improved upon. In addition to the staining or colouring, it is but reasonable to suppose various ornaments would soon be added by people to whom many of the fine arts were so familiar. We have direct testimony of the adoption of impressed gold ornaments, and the DIPTYCH, to which we shall now refer, proves that sculptured figures and other carved embellishment were very extensively introduced.

To enter fully into a description of the nature, form, and circumstances connected with the Diptych, cannot, from its great extent, here be effected. Gori has filled three folio volumes on the subject, and to his learned work we must be content to refer the curious in this matter. They have been classed under two descriptions, the profane and sacred. The former

ᶜ Edinb. Review, 1, 256.

will here engage our attention, reserving the latter to
the next chapter, as coming properly under the period
devoted to the consideration of the bindings, more
immediately connected with monastic and religious
institutions.

The name is from the *duplice*, or two-leaved *pugillaria*, consisting, like it, of two boards covered with
wax, on which the characters were marked with the
stylus. They were of similar character but different
application ; the pugillaria being small, as before described, for private memorandums ; whilst the Diptych,
of large dimensions, more especially appertained to
the public acts of the consuls, magistrates, and other
functionaries. They were generally composed of
ebony or box-wood, connected together by two or
more hinges. They were then embellished with
carved ivory, and frequently with silver, gold, and
precious stones, riveted very closely to the wood, and
finished with the utmost elegance and taste. The
names of the consuls, and the titles they respectively
bore, generally in a contracted form, were inscribed
upon them. The nature of the carving, &c., was
much alike in design, though of varied execution.
Of twelve described by Gori, very little difference
exists, being full-length portraits of the consuls, and
compartments exhibiting the peculiar games and
amusements of the people. The description of one,
which he designates the " DIPTYCHON LEODIENSE,"
will fully illustrate the nature of their extensive and
elaborate ornament. Seated in the centre of each

board is a portrait of the consul, holding in one hand
a baton, and in the other, upraised, a purse, as if in
the act of throwing it to some victor in the games.
Above are three miniature portraits, various other
ornaments, and the inscription. Below, on one board,
is a representation of a combat with wild beasts. On
the other are two men, leading out horses for the race,
and beneath them a group, with a ludicrous representation of two other men exhibiting the strength of
their endurance of pain by allowing crabs to fasten
on their noses. The frame-work and general detail
are filled up with the best effect and proportion. The
inscription on the first side is

FL ANASTASIVS PAVL PROVS
SAVINIANVS POMP ANAST

and on the second,

V INL COM DOMEST EQVIT
ET CONS ORD

This he pronounces to refer to ANASTASIUS, " Consul
Orientis," A. D. 517, and his name and title, as
*Anastasius Paulus Probus Sabianus Pompeius, vir
ilustris comes domesticorum equitum, et consul or-
dinarius.*[u]

The inscriptions on several are of a like character,
but one, the " Diptychon Bituricense," relates to the
above *Anastasius*, the inscription being nearly the

[u] Gori's Thesaurus Vet. Diptychorum, i. 4.

E

same. This latter appears to have found its way
into the royal library, Paris, as it is described by Dr.
Dibdin, in his Tour,ᵛ as well as a letter inserted in
it, written by a Mons. Mercier, on the subject of
Diptychs, taken principally from Gori.

For the better understanding of this part of the
subject, an illustration of one from the library of the
Vatican is presented. It refers to the Consul Boethius,
who flourished anno 487. Its character is seen in
the engraving. A similar figure, seated, with the
purse and upraised hand, is on the other side, which
bears part of the inscription,

NARMANLBOETHIVSVCETINL
EXPPPVSECCONSORDETPATRIC

and which Gori, in a lengthened description, inter-
prets as referring to " *Manlius Boethius consul ordi-
narius et patricius.*"

Of this description of ornament did many of the
side covers of books of former times consist, as we
shall have occasion soon to speak, and there can be
but little doubt that the Greeks and Romans were
profuse in this addition to the beauty of their literary
treasures.   Montfaucon,ʷ in his researches relative to
ancient literature, confirms many of the facts that
have been brought forward. He says, " the Greeks,
after the custom of the present day, fastened together
the leaves of their books, distributed into threes and

NARMANIBOETHIVSVCELINI

FAC-SIMILE OF AN IVORY DIPTYCH,
IN THE LIBRARY OF THE VATICAN, ROME.

fours, covered them with calf, or some other skin
generally thicker. They strengthened the upper and
lower part, where the book is more embellished, with
a wooden tablet glued to the side in order that the
leaves might adhere together more firmly." And
Schwarz[x] that the "books of the Romans, about the
time of the Christian era, were covered at one time
with red and yellow leather, at another time with
green leather; at one time with purple, at another
with silver, at another with gold."

The authorities cited, and existing specimens of
ancient workmanship referred to in illustration of the
subject, amply prove that the ancients were as profuse in the embellishment of their books, as they were
careful in their preparation. They had also their
large paper copies, and what may be called their hot-
pressed compositions, still notable in our day, being
twice polished with pumice.[y] That the art must have
arrived at a considerable degree of perfection, is further
confirmed by the accounts of the number of volumes
contained in their public libraries, and which of necessity would require the protection binding gives, to
preserve them from injury. The earliest notice of a
repository for records is the house of the rolls in
Babylon, referred to in Ezra, vi. 2. In the celebrated
Alexandrian library, consisting of seven hundred
thousand volumes, and the one subsequently formed
at Constantinople, of upwards of one hundred and

[x] De Ornament. Lib Vet. Disp. iii. 166.——[y] Notes to
Catullus, Ode xix.

E 2

twenty thousand, doubtless not only the common purpose of preservation would be attended to, but elegance and embellishment studied. Zonarus relates
that among other treasures in the latter, there was a
roll one hundred feet long made of a dragon's gut
or intestine, on which Homer s Iliad and Odyssey were
written in letters of gold. Of the splendour of the
libraries of the Romans, it is reported that that of
the younger Gordian, at Rome, was paved with marble,
and ornamented with gold; that the walls were
covered with glass and ivory, and that the armouries
and desks were made of ebony and silver.[a]

Nor do books in the time of the ancients appear to
have been so scarce as in periods nearer our own
day they will be seen to have been; for in addition
to their numerous public libraries, we find many
notices of those of private individuals; as that of
Lucullus, mentioned by Plutarch; of one at Tusculum
named by Cicero; of that of Appellico the Teian, at
Athens, which Sylla took to Rome; of that of the
Pisos found at Herculanæum,[b] and o[c] numerous others
containing large collections of books. The testimony
of Seneca, Cicero, and Pliny, relative to the pleasure
they derived from their libraries, also shows that
books were comparatively plentiful. They were at
that time an article of commerce. Catullus,[c] in an
Ode to Calvus, who had presented him with some

---

[a] Warton's Eng. Poetry, i. 104. ——[a] Astle's Writing, introduction vii.——[b] Herculanensia, 91.——[c] Ode xiv.

despicable authors, promises him a return of others
as worthless, in search of which he says

> " Let but the morn appear, I'll run
> To ev'ry *book-stall* in the town.

Pollux speaks of booksellers' shops as being among
the parts of sea-port towns.[d] We also find mention
of stands for the sale of books in such places ;[e] and
Martial describes a bookseller's shop as having all
the pillars or posts inscribed with the titles of the
vendible books, the best being kept in the *upper nidus*,
and the inferior in those below.[f] That these *libraria*,
or booksellers shops, existed in almost every large
city or town under the Roman sway, is abundantly
confirmed by Horace,[g] Pliny,[h] Cicero, and others.
This trade in books must have given employment to
a great number of BIBLIOPEGI or BOOKBINDERS, who
were also called *librorum concinnatores, compactores,*
and who appear to have had under their direction the
glutinatores, mentioned in Cicero's fourth epistle to
Atticus.

Taking a review of this part of our subject, it may
be pronounced in conclusion that a system of bookbinding was known to the Greeks and Romans very
little, if any, inferior to our own ; that in elegance
and finish, as in every other matter where taste was
required, and in which they so much excelled, they
would not be deficient ; but that from the continued

[d] Book vii. 33.——[e] Dionisius of Halicarnassus, x. 5.——
Epigram 1. 118.——[g] Epist. i. 20.——[h] ix Epist. 11.——
Philippic xi. 9.

wear to which the cover of a book is subject, and more particularly to the total destruction of all the Roman libraries by the successive irruptions of the Northern armies into the Western empire, and the sacking of Alexandria and Constantinople by the Saracens and Turks, no *perfect* remains of bookbinding as it was in their time, has come down to ours. The state and progress of the art, during another era, will be the object of our endeavours now to illustrate.

CHAPTER III.

MONASTIC AND OTHER BINDINGS UP TO THE INVENTION OF PRINTING.

For upwards of two thousand years it has been shown in the preceding chapter that the Art of Book-binding, by means of attaching the leaves to the back and affixing boards to the sides, has been practised, the addition of embellishment following in its train as a matter of taste, if not of necessity. Having, as we trust satisfactorily, established these facts, it will now be necessary to pass to the consideration of the subject as connected with the monastic institutions of Europe, when, from the annals of religious communities, and the appearance of bindings of the twelfth and thirteenth centuries, we shall not only be able to show what was the state of the art at that time ; but, reasoning from what we find it then to be, confirm what has been advanced as to the knowledge of it possessed by the ancients.

It will be first necessary to advert to the state of literature and scarcity of books in this and other countries of Europe in early times, being partly illustrative of the progress of the art, connected as the making and binding of books will now be found to be. Before the invention of paper from linen, books were so scarce and dear, as to be beyond the reach of all but the rich, and it may reasonably be computed that the price of books was a hundred fold their present value. Though the materials of which they were made had been as cheap and as plentiful as paper is at present, the labour of multiplying copies in manuscript would always have kept them comparatively scanty. Hence learning was almost exclusively confined to people of rank. The papyrus was in most general use; but when the Saracens conquered Egypt in the seventh century it could no longer be procured. Parchment, the only substance for writing which then remained, was so difficult to be obtained that it was customary to erase the characters of antiquity, and Sophocles or Tacitus were obliged to resign the parchment to missals, homilies, and the Golden Legend.[a] In this manner many of the best works of antiquity were for ever lost, though some have in late times been recovered, from the imperfect manner the first writing was erased.[b] History records many facts which place in a very striking light the scarcity and consequent value of books during the dark ages. Private persons seldom possessed any books at all, and even distinguished mo-

[a] Gibbon's Rome, v. 380.——[b] Edinb. Review, xlviii. 353.

nasteries could in general boast of no more than a
single missal.   The collections which the ancients
possessed did not in these times exist, for the libraries,
particularly those of Italy, which abounded in innumerable and inestimable treasures of literature, were, as
has been before referred to, every where destroyed by
the precipitate rage and undistinguishing violence of
the northern armies.   Of the rarity of books, Warton,
in the second Dissertation to his History of English
Poetry, has given a long account.   During this period
the monasteries principally became the depositories of
science.   They were more tranquil than the rest of
the world, and thither the arts fled for refuge ; artists
became monks and monks became artists, the manuscripts and illuminations executed by them, which are
still preserved to us, attest their dexterity and skill
in designing and executing the most beautiful and
complex subjects.[c]   And it is evident from various
accounts left us, that the religious were not only the
writers and illuminators, but also the binders of books
in the times of the Saxons, which they continued to
practise up to the invention of printing.   The monks
and students in monasteries were the principal la-
bourers in this business, and it was part of the sacrist's
duty to bind and clasp the books used for the service
of the church.[d]   A book, usually known by the name
of *Textus Sanctus Cuthberti*, preserved in the Cotto-
nian Library (Nero, D. IV.) is a fine specimen of

[c] Specimens of Ancient Sculpture, ii. —— [d] Warton, ii. 244.

Saxon caligraphy and decoration of the seventh century. It was written by Eadfrid, bishop of Durham, and
Ethelwold, his successor, executed the illuminations,
the capitals, and other illustrations, with infinite labour
and elegance. Bilfrid, a monk of Durham, covered
the book, and adorned it with gold and silver plates
set with precious stones.   These particulars are
related by Aldred, the Saxon glossator, at the end of
St. John's gospel.   Simon, of Durham, or Turgot,
tells us that the cover of it was ornamented "foren-
secis geminis et auro."   Many curious tales are
related concerning this book ; amongst others, Turgot
gravely asserts, that when the monks of Lindisfarn
were removing from thence, to avoid the depredations
of the Danes, the vessel wherein they were embarked
oversetting, this book, which they were transporting
with them, fell into the sea.   Through the merits
of St. Cuthbert, the sea ebbing much further than
usual, it was found upon the sands, above three miles
from the shore, without having received injury from
the water.[e]   The original binding has been replaced
by a russia covering, having been, most likely, de
spoiled of its ornaments at the period of the reformation.   We find also tnat Dagæus, a monk who
flourished in Ireland in the early part of the sixth
century, was a skilful caligraphist, and manufactured
and ornamented binding, in gold, silver, and precious
stones. He died A. D. 587.   Ethelwolf, in a metri-

[e] Astle's Writing, 101.

cal epistle to Egbert, at that time resident in Ireland, with a view of collecting MSS. extols one Ultan, an Irish monk, for his talents in adorning books. Herman, one of the Norman bishops of Salisbury, about the year 1080, not only wrote and illuminated books, but also bound them.[g] Some of the classics were early written and bound in the English monasteries. Henry, a Benedictine monk of Hyde abbey, near Winchester, transcribed, in the year 1178, Terence, Boetius, Suetonius, and Claudian, which he bound in one book, and formed the brazen bosses of the covers with his own hands.[h]

For the purposes above enumerated every great abbey appropriated a room, which was called the SCRIPTORIUM. Here several persons were constantly employed in transcribing not only the service books for the choir, but books for the library; and binding them. Ingulphus, of the abbey of Croyland, speaking of the lending of books, says "Our books, as well the smaller unbound volumes, as the larger ones which are bound, we altogether forbid."[i] The custom of making this one good use of convents and of Christian societies, was derived from very early times. About the year 220 Alexander, bishop of Jerusalem, built there a library for the preservation of the epistles of the learned. And Origen was assisted in the production of his works by several notaries, who

[f] O'Conor's Rerum Hebernicarum, clxxvii. ——[g] Mon. Angl. iii. 275. ——[h] Warton, i. cxliv. dis. 2. ——[i] Ing. ap. Gale, 104.

wrote down in turn that which he uttered.[k]   For the
support of the Scriptorium, estates were often granted.
That at St. Edmondsbury was endowed with two mills.
The tithes of a rectory were appropriated to the
cathedral convent of St. Swithin, at Winchester, in
the year 1171.   Many other instances of this species
of transaction occur.   About the year 790, Charle-
magne granted an unlimited right of hunting to the
abbot and monks of Sithin, for making their gloves
and girdles of the skins of the deer they killed, and
covers for their books.   Nigel, in the year 1160, gave
the monks of Ely two churches, *ad libros faciendos*.
R. de Paston granted to Bromholm. abbey, in
Norfolk, 12d. per annum, a' rent charge on his lands,
to keep their books in repair.   These employments
appear to have been diligently practised at Croyland,
for Ingulphus relates that when the abbey was burnt
in the year 1091, seven hundred volumes were con-
sumed.   Large sums were disbursed for grails,
legends, and other service-books for the choir of the
chapel of Winchester college, as is shown by a roll of
John Morys, the warden, an.xx. Richard II.A.D.1397.
It appears, in this case, that they bought the parchment, and hired persons to do the business of writing,
illuminating, noting, and binding, within the walls of
the college.   The books were covered with deer-skin.
As Item in vj pellibus *cervinis* emptis pro libris pre-
dictis cooperiendis, xiijs. iiijd.   The monks, as has
been before remarked, were skilful illuminators.

[k] Eccl. Hist. of Eusebius Pamphilus, book vi. c. 20.

They were also *taught* to *bind books*.   In the year
1277, these constitutions were given to the Benedictine monasteries of the province of Canterbury :
"Abbates monachos suos claustrales, loco operis manu-
alis, secundem suam habilitatem cæteris occupationi-
bus deputent : in studendo, libros scribendo, corri-
gendo, illuminando, ligando." That the students
and monks were the binders of books, is further confirmed by a note in the first page of a manuscript Life
of Concubramis.   " Ex conjunctione (ligatura)
dompui Wyllelmi Edys monasterii B. Mariæ S. Mod-
wenæ virginis de Burton super Trent monachi, dum
esset studens Oxoniæ, A. D. 1517.[1]   Haymo de
Hethe, in the original endowment of Chalk, in Kent,
in 1327, compelled the vicars to be at the expense of
binding their missals, " *libros etiam ligari faciet.*"[m]

The multiplying of books, with their bindings and
decorations, were almost solely confined to the religious houses in the early ages of christianity, and
that it continued to be so until the invention of printing there is abundant proof.   In one of John of
Trittenheim's (abbot of Spanheim) exhortations, in
the year 1486, after many injunctions against idleness,
he observes that he has " diminished their labour out
of the monastery, lest by working badly you should
only add to your sins, and have enjoined on you the
manual labour of writing and *binding* books." And
again, urging them to the duty, he says—" It is true

Warton, i. cxlvi. dis. 2.——[m] Archæologia, xi. 362.

that the industry of the printing art, lately, in our
day, discovered at Mentz, produces many volumes
every day; but it is impossible for us, depressed as
we are by poverty, to buy them all."[n] From their
scarcity, they were more curious of their books than
we are. They therefore were extremely anxious for
their preservation, but unfortunately that which
appeared likely to protect them for ages, often proved
their destruction. The side covers were formed of
wood, which tended to facilitate the ravages of the
worm, and when not of a good quality the edges
soon got damaged, and the books suffered considerably. These wooden covers doubtless were at first
perfectly smooth and unadorned, but as the contents
of the work would frequently be of importance, it may
reasonably be supposed that, like the people of still
earlier times, the owners would decorate the exterior
according to the extent of their esteem for the book.
Hence originated the art of embellishment upon the
side covers.

The earliest specimens of the external decoration of
books that have been preserved to our day, is doubtless those of the DIPTYCH, one class of which have
been described. We shall now refer to those of a
sacred character, or such as were connected with the
affairs and administration of the early churches. They
were in every respect, except the ornament, like those
referred to at page 36. This ornament consisted of
carved illustrations of passages in the lives of the

[n] Br. Mag. x. 128.

Saviour, the Virgin, the Apostles, and the saints of the
Romish church; some of them bearing in compartments as many as twenty-two subjects.   Gori has
devoted the whole of his third volume to them.   The
earliest specimens are of rude workmanship, but as
the church progressed in prosperity, the same elegance
of finish we have had occasion before to remark, is
found upon these.   One subject of frequent occurrence,
is the Saviour, seated in the act of teaching as here
represented.

This occupies the centre of the board; the corners are variously filled up with the four evangelists, their emblems, or subjects of religious import.

The Royal Library at Munich contains the finest specimens of this description of book ornament in the world. The British Museum exhibits very few, and those not of a splendid character. The late Mr. Douce possessed a number of diptychs, the particulars of which have been given by Sir S. R. Meyrick, to whom they were bequeathed.° One of them, of the time of Edward the First, he says, is in ivory, and when open, measures eleven inches and three quarters long, and eleven wide. In front of the subjects, which are in alto-relievo, are twelve trefoiled arches within pointed ones, arranged in two tiers, the upper row having pediments with crockets and finials. The first subject is the Annunciation; then the interview between Mary and Elizabeth. Next the angels appearing to the shepherds to tell them of the birth of Christ. One of these last is beating a tabor with a drumstick, and another playing on the bagpipes. In front of them are Joseph, the Virgin, and Child. Then three kings on horseback, their bridles made half their length of chain, and three on foot, come into the presence of one sitting on his throne (probably Herod), attended by his mace-bearer, announce their intention of taking the presents they bear to the infant Jesus. Next, the Virgin appears seated

° Gent.'s Mag. new series, v. 585.

on a Gothic chair, being crowned by a descending
angel, bearing the child on her lap, before whom appear
three of the kings with their presents, one kneeling
and taking off his crown with one hand, as he makes
the offering with the other.　Lastly, Herod's cruelty,
the soldiers wearing the cervelliere over the capuchon
of mail, and surcoats.　On the outside it is ornamented with foliage.

The acts of the religious rulers, like those of the
consuls, gifts to the church, &c. were noted in these
diptychs.[p]　Montfaucon states the names of the
bishops were carefully registered, or erased, according to the purity or immorality of their lives.[q]

The ornament seen on the diptych soon became
common on the choice *books* of the church, and the
plain wooden cover was adorned with all the ingenuity
that wealth and taste could bestow.　The libraries on
the continent are much richer in gems of this description than our own country, and some specimens
have been described by Dr. Dibdin[r] with great
minuteness.　St. Jerom, who flourished in the fourth
century, refers to the splendour of many books in his
time.[s]　A book of the Gospels, translated by Ulphilas,
bishop of Moesia, A. D. 370, was called the "Silver
Book of Ulphilas," because bound in massy silver.[t]
Another copy presented by the emperor Justin to
pope Hormisda, between the years 518 and 523, was

[p] Gori Thesaurus Vet. Dipt. i. 2.——[q] Palæog. Græcæ, 34.
——[r] Bibliographical Tour, iii. 262 and 460.——[s] Astle's
Writing, 196.——[t] Ibid. 87.

bound in plates ot gold and enriched with precious
stones, to the weight of fifteen pounds. Leo III.,
who was raised to the pontificate in 795, gave to
various churches copies of the Gospels, alike splendidly
ornamented. The abbot Angilbert, on the restoration
of the abbey of St. Riquier, A. D. 814, presented to
it a copy of the Gospels, in silver plates, " marvel
lously adorned with gold and precious stones.
Another copy, written in letters of gold and silver,
and bound in gold, enriched with gems, was presented
to his church by Hincmar, on becoming archbishop
of Rheims in 845. The emperor Michael, about the
year 855, sent as a present to St. Peter's, a Gospel
of most pure gold, with divers precious stones.
Everhard, count of Friuli, bequeathed by will, A. D.
861, to his children, his Bible, and a number of other
books, among which a Gospel bound in gold, another
in silver, and another in ivory. In 1022, the emperor Henry II., on recovering from illness, at the
monastery of Monte Casino, presented to it a copy
of the Gospels, covered on one side with most pure
gold, and most precious gems. Returning the same
year into Germany, he had an interview with Robert,
king of France, but of all the rich presents offered by
that king, the emperor accepted only a copy of the
Gospels, bound in gold and precious stones. Desi-
derius, who became abbot of the above monastery in
1058, provided it with many costly books; and the
empress Agnes made many rich gifts to the church,
and among the rest, a copy of the Gospels, with one

side of cast silver, with chased or embossed work,
very beautifully gilt."

These specimens will suffice to give an idea of the
labour and expense expended on the external decoration of books at a very early period of the history
of Europe.   But to return more particularly to the
productions of the monks and religious of our own
country, we shall find that in their progress they did
not lose their ancient reputation.   We have before
described the book of St. Cuthbert, and other works.
The next earliest is a Latin Psalter considered to be
the oldest extant in England, and thus described
by Moule.'   " The original book upon which all our
kings, from Henry I. to Edward VI., took the coronation oath, is now in the library of a gentleman in
Norfolk.   It is a MS. of the four Evangelists, written
on vellum, the form and beauty of the letters nearly
approaching to Roman capitals.   It appears to have
been written and bound for the coronation of Henry
I.   The original binding, which is still in a perfect
state, consists of two oaken boards, nearly an inch
thick, fastened together with stout thongs of leather,
and the corners defended with large bosses of brass.
On the right-hand side, as the book is opened, of the
outer cover is a crucifix of brass, double gilt, which
was kissed by the kings upon their inauguration ; and
the whole is fastened together by a strong clasp of
brass, fixed to a broad piece of leather secured with

u Papers on the Dark Ages, No. xiii.—Br. Mag. ix. 249. ——
Bibliotheca Heraldica, 493.

two brass pins." This book is now in the library of the Duke of Buckingham at Stowe. It was formerly entered in the Exchequer as a little book with a crucifix. The crucifix is about six or eight inches in height, and the workmanship rather clumsy. A drawing of it by Vertue, is in the collection of the Society of Antiquaries." Another MS. Gospel, partly Latin and partly Saxon, in the British Museum (Cotton MSS. Titus D. xxvii.) is also bound with oaken boards, one being inlaid with pieces of carved ivory, which is supposed to have been executed at a later period, probably from the piety of some subsequent owner. They are however very curious and deserving of explicit notice. The first consists of our Saviour, with an angel above him : the second of the Virgin with Christ in her lap—the Virgin is in half length : the third is a small whole length of Joseph with an angel above. A gilt *nimbus* is round the head of each, but that which encircles the Virgin is perfect ; and the compartment in which she appears (about 5 inches high) is twice the size of each of the others. The draperies throughout are good. It is altogether a choice specimen of ancient binding. This mode of external ornament is further illustrated by the following description of two books by Mr. Astle, in a paper on crosses and crucifixes. " A booke of Gospelles garnished and wrought with antique worke of silver and gilte with an image of the crucifix, with Mary and John, poiz together

" Dibdin's Bib. Decam. ii. 434.——ˣ Ibid.

cccxxij. oz." In the Jewel House in the Tower "a
booke of gold enameled, clasped with a rubie, having
on th' one syde a crosse of dyamounts, and vj. other
dyamounts, and th' other side a flower de luce of
dyamounts, and iiij. rubies with a pendante of white
sapphires, and the armes of Englande. Which booke
is garnished with small emeraldes and rubies hanging
to a chayne pillar fashion set with xv knottes, everie
one conteyning iij. rubies (one lacking)."[y]

It was also usual in early times to engrave the arms
of the owner on the clasps which were generally
attached to books. Eleanor, duchess of Gloucester,
mentions in her will, in 1339, " a Chronicle of France,"
in French, with two clasps of silver, enamelled with
the arms of the Duke of Burgoyne; a book containing the Psalter, Primer, and other devotions, with
two clasps of gold enamelled with her arms; a French
Bible in two volumes, with two gold clasps enamelled
with the arms of France; and a Psalter richly illuminated, with the clasps of gold enamelled with white
swans, and the arms of my lord and father enamelled
on the clasps.[z] Among the books in the inventory
of the effects of Sir John Fastolfe, were two " Mys-
sayles closyd with sylver," and a " Sauter claspyd
with sylver, and my maysters is armys and my ladyes
ther uppon."[a]

The Bedford Missal is, perhaps, as splendid a specimen of the taste and ingenuity of the monks, as any

<hr />

[y] Archæologia xiii. 220.——[z] Nicolas' Test. Vetusta, i. 148.
—— [a] Archæol. xxi. 276.

extant. It contains fifty-nine large miniatures, occupying nearly the whole page, and above a thousand small ones, in circles of about an inch in diameter, displayed in elegant borders of golden foliage, with variegated flowers, &c. Among the portraits are whole-length ones of John, duke of Bedford, regent of France in the reign of Henry VI., and of his duchess. The volume measures eleven inches by seven and a half in width, and two inches and a half in thickness. It is bound in crimson velvet with gold clasps, whereon are engraved the arms of Harley, Cavendish, and Hollis quarterly. The duke of Bedford presented it to his nephew Henry VI.[b] It was bought of the Somerset family, by Harley, second earl of Oxford; from whom it came to the late duchess of Portland, at whose sale Mr. Edwards became the owner for 215 guineas. It was sold again in 1815 to the marquis of Blandford for 687*l*. 15*s*. Sir John Tobin is now the possessor.

These may be pronounced as fair general specimens of the talent of the ancient European Bookbinders, time, damp, the worm, and religious zeal, having worked the destruction of the coverings of nearly all the early manuscripts; though to the latter must be attributed not only the scarcity of proof of what the bindings of these talented monks and artists were, but the entire loss of the books also. The mistaken zeal, enthusiasm, and bigotry of the early leaders of

[b] Horne's Bibliography, i. 302, and Nichol's Illust. vi. 296.

the reformation, or of those they employed, swept
away without distinction the works of the learned
with the books of devotion preserved in the religious
houses, and deprived the world doubtless of many
treasures now unknown. With these the bindings were
of course destroyed, and even in cases where the book
may have been preserved, the cupidity of many to
whom the task of visiting the religious establishments
was assigned, would lead them to divest them of the
valuable ornaments with which we have shown many
were enriched and decorated. Not only were the
libraries completely sacked, but the huge volumes
which contained the ancient services, and abounded
in all the churches and monasteries, were destroyed
without mercy, ardently and enthusiastically. Many
of these had been brought direct from Rome, where a
great manufactory of such works had for some centuries existed. An immense volume was laid upon
the *lutrin*, or reading-desk, in the middle of the choir,
and the letters and musical notes, which accompanied
the words, were of such an enormous magnitude,
and so black, that they could be read by the canons,
as they sat in their stalls, at as great a distance, and
with as much ease, as an inscription on a monument.
These ponderous volumes lay unmolested on the desk,
or at the utmost were only carried to the adjoining
sacristy, and were a part of the furniture, and almost
of the fixtures, of the churches; they were exempt
from injury and accident, and were frequently therefore of great antiquity, having been constructed in

very remote times, when manuscripts of value were plentiful.[c] They were garnished with corners of brass, with bosses, and brass nails, to preserve the bindings from injury in being rubbed on the desk or pulpit, and protected from dust by massive clasps. Some, when very large, were, for further protection, laid upon rollers. The nature and extent of these additions are shown in an illumination of a MS. of the fifteenth century, in the Royal Library, Paris, from which the following is taken.

The accumulation, though slowly, had, in a great number of years, led to the formation of many considerable libraries in the houses of the religious at the period of the reformation.[d] Of the extent of the devastation and frightful havoc then committed a writer of the time gives an account. Speaking of the destruction of books, he indignantly says, " Never had we been offended for the loss of our libraries, being so many in number, and in so desolate places for the more part, if the chief monuments and most notable works of our most excellent witers had been

[c] Edinb. Review, xlviii. 96.——[d] Leland's Collectanea, i. 109.

preserved. If there had been in every shire of England but one *solempne* library, to the preservation of those noble works, and preferment of good learning in our posterity, it had been yet somewhat. But to destroy all without consideration, is, and will be, unto England for ever, a most horrible infamy among the grave seniors of other nations. A great number of them which purchased those superstitious mansions, reserved of those library-books, some to serve the jakes, some to scour their candlesticks, and some to rub their boots ; some they sold to the grocers and soap-sellers ; some they sent over sea to the *bookbinders*, not in small numbers but at times whole ships full, to the wondering of the foreign nations. Yea, the universities of this realm are not all clear of this detestable fact. But cursed is that belly which seeketh to be fed with such ungodly gains, and shameth his natural country. I know a merchant man, which shall at this time be nameless, that bought the contents of *two noble libraries* for *forty shillings* price ; a shame it is to be spoken. This stuff hath he occupied in the stead of grey paper, by the space of more than ten years, and yet he hath store enough for as many years to come!"[e]

With these facts before us it need not be matter of surprise how few specimens of bookbinding, prior to the introduction of printing, now exist. Previous extracts have shown the early adoption of wooden boards as

[e] Bale's Preface to Leland's Journey, 1549.

side covers, for books, by the monastic binders
Every means were used for their preservation, hence
strength and durability were most studied.   They
sewed them on pieces of skin or parchment; and even
carried their precaution so far as to protect each sheet
externally and internally with a slip of parchment, to
prevent the thread, with which the book was sewn,
from cutting the paper, and to protect the back from
injury.   When the boards were first covered, it
appears that a common parchment or vellum, made
from the skin of the deer, was used.   Richard Chan-
dos, bishop of Chichester, mentions in his will, so
early as the year 1253, a " Bible, with a rough cover
of skin," and bequeaths it to William de Selsey.[f]
Another proof of the adoption of this covering occurs
in the "Accounts of the Household of Edward I. and
II.," contained in four MS. volumes presented to the
Society of Antiquaries, by Sir Ashton Lever; which
were in the original binding of calf-skin, dressed like
parchment with the hair on, and razures of the hair
made for writing the inscription.[g]   Elizabeth de
Burgh, in the year 1355, by will left " to my hall,
called Clare Hall, Cambridge,"   among other books,
one missal, covered with white leather or hide, and
one good Bible covered with black leather.[h]   More
expensive ornament followed, as has been shown.
Velvet was long the material used for the *covers* of

[f] Nicolas Testamenta Vetusta, ii. 762.——[g] Archæologiæ, vii.
118-19.——[h] Nicolas, i. 58.

the best works.   The Bible, when first translated into
Latin, was divided into four or six parts.   In the will
of Richard (Sanctus), bishop of Chichester, he bequeathed to the four orders of friars, each one part,
(1258) " glossatam," which means with marginal
notes.   In the next century the Bible was translated
into French, illuminated, with a commentary, and
bound in two volumes covered with velvet, with clasps
of gold, enamelled with the arms of the prince or
nobleman at whose expense the MS. was made.
Psalters were more common.   Missals, as has been
before remarked, were so splendid as to have miniatures in every page, and were wrought with jewels
on the covers of the velvet.[i]   The wills of the
nobles and rich of this country, in times when it was
the custom to leave books as legacies to friends and
ecclesiastical bodies, however, furnish the best evidence of the use of velvet as a cover for books in very
early times.   In the will of Lady Fitzhugh, A.D. 1427,
several books, &c., are thus bequeathed :— " Als so I
wyl yat my son William have a Ryng with a dyamond
and my son Geffray a gretter, and my son Rob't a
sauter covered with rede velvet, and my doghter
Mariory a primer cou'ed in Rede, and my doghter
Darcy a sauter cou'ed in blew, and my doghter Malde
Eure a prim' cou'd in blew."[k]   Eleanor, countess of
Arundel, left by will to Ann, wife of her nephew,

[i] Nicolas, i. xxvii. Notes.——[k] Wills and Inventories, part
i. Surtees Society, and Nicolas, i. 213.

Maurice Berkeley, a book of Matins covered with velvet. This was in the year 1455 ; and in 1480, a similar bequest was made to her daughter, by Ann, duchess of Buckingham, of a primer covered with purple velvet, with clasps of silver gilt.[l]

These records prove velvet to have been used as a cover for books long before the time usually assigned to it, and shows that every variety of colour was adopted according to the subject matter of the contents of the volume. This was particularly the case a century or two earlier, for among the courtesies of love in chivalric times, the present of books from knights to ladies was not forgotton, and it more often happened than monkish austerity approved of, that a volume *bound in sacred guise*, contained not a series of hymns to the Virgin, but a variety of amatory effusions to a terrestrial mistress.[m]

The will of Walter, lord Hungerford, proves the use also of coloured cloths for binding at an early period. He bequeathed in 1449, to Lady Margaret, wife of Sir Robert Hungerford his son, " my best Legend of the lives of the saints in French, and covered with *red cloth.*[n]

The art of bookbinding, it is seen, both as respects style, and variety of material for the covers, was far advanced at the period that witnessed the invention of printing. The details of its history for a century after that event, may be pronounced the history,

[l] Nicolas, i. 279, 357.——[m] Mill's History of Chivalry, i. 42. —— [n] Nicolas, i. 258.

making allowance for the improvements the greater number of books and consequent field for exertion would produce, of at least a like period before.   We proceed to trace it under new circumstances, attested by numerous records and notices of writers of days gone by,—illustrated and corroborated by specimens of bindings that have withstood the havoc of time.

CHAPTER IV.

ENGLISH BINDING AND BINDERS, FROM THE INVENTION
OF PRINTING TO THE EIGHTEENTH CENTURY, MORE
PARTICULARLY AS RELATES TO MATERIALS AND FI-
NISH.

THE multiplication of manuscripts, which the introduction of paper, made from linen, into Europe, occasioned, caused a considerable reduction in their
price, and contributed essentially to the diffusion of
knowledge. Learning had already begun to revive,
and to be cultivated with considerable ardour, when
the invention of printing by John Gutenburgh, of
Mayence, or Mentz, about the year 1438, gave a new
stimulus to the human mind, and formed the most important era to the history of literature and civilization.[a] It drew forth learning from libraries and convents, and, by increasing the number of books, placed
them within the reach of all. The avenues of science
were thus thrown open to every one, and volumes of
information which had before existed in costly manuscripts, were now in every hand. No retrogression

[a] Gibbon.

in knowledge or the arts, could ever more take place, recorded as it now became in a thousand ways, spreading abroad the intelligence, improvements, and inventions of the more skilful, and making them alike the common property of the whole community.

What printing became to the other arts, binding now, in an especial manner, became to the productions of the press. And, that the practisers of the art were fully sensible of this is shown by the firm way the bindings of early printed books, which are still preserved, are executed. And to this care we may attribute the existence of so many specimens of early typography, for if the slight and careless manner, in which some bindings of a later date have been executed, had at that time been common, it is but reasonable to suppose, that we should also have to regret the loss of many of those specimens we now possess.

The art of printing was introduced into England by William Caxton in 1473, and his press fully established in Westminster Abbey in 1477.[b] The early English printers, however, did not make much progress, for it appears that an act was passed in the year 1483, authorizing " strangers repairing unto this realm to bring printed and written books, to sell at their pleasure." Books were at first printed either in large or small folio, or at least quartos ; the smaller sizes were not in use till some time after the inven-

[b]Ame's Typograph. Antiq. i. 3.

tion of printing, if at all, certainly but rarely previous to A. D. 1480.[c] At this time too, and long after, every process belonging to a printed book, from the punch to the *binding*, was included under the general denomination of *printing*.[d]   Of the early English *bookbinders*, consequently, very little is known, and that only from their connection with the printing branch of the profession. Thus we find that Wynkyn de Worde, the successor of Caxton, left by will, legacies, to Nowel, the *bookbinder* in Shoe Lane, and to Alard, bookbinder, his servant.[e]   This Nowel, doubtless, was what is now called a *chamber binder*,— that is, doing work for the bookseller and printer, and perhaps at that time wholly employed by Wynkyn de Worde. John Reynes, at the George, in St. Paul's Church-Yard, about the year 1527, was an eminent publisher and *binder*.[f]   To these, in further confirmation, may be added, Michael Lobley and William Hill,[g] living in St. Paul's Church-Yard, 1531—1536, as also "Toye, the bookbinder," named as engaged in search for the printers of a work against the government of the church, about 1550.[h]

Of the progressive improvement in bookbinding and the materials with which the books were covered, the public libraries of Europe, and especially, as will be seen in another chapter, the royal library at Paris, exhibit many specimens. Manuscript books,

[c] Horne's Int. to Bibliography, i. 291.——[d] Hansard's Typographia, 334.——[e] Ame's Typographica Antiquities, i. 120. ——[f] Ibid. i. 413.——[g] Ibid. ii. 756.—— Ibid. i. 569.

and those printed many years after the invention of
printing, were variously decorated in binding. David
Casley, deputy librarian to Ccorge II., speaking on
the subject, says, " The very covers of a great many
MSS. are curiosities, there having been different
ways of binding books in different ages : and some
have happened to have been bound with so good
material as to have lasted a great while, which may
be proved by several books which, upon examination
appear to have been but once bound."[i]

The common ccver for early printed works doubtless remained, as for MSS. in monastic times, a kind
of parchment or forrel. But for the books of the
noble and rich, as has been shown, a considerable
degree of elegance had been adopted. Velvet was
the most usual, and in this degree of luxury the
poorer classes of readers now also indulged. Chaucer,
in describing the " Clerke of Oxenforde," says—

" ꝗor ꜧym was leuer to ꜧabe at ꜧys beddes ꜧeed
Twenty bookes cladde wyth blacke or reed."[k]

And in "An inventory of English Books, of John
Paston, made the 5th day of November, in the ——
year of the reign of Edward IV." we find particularized :

Item—A *black* book with the Legend of . . . . Lady sans
Merci.
Item—A *red* book, that Percival Robsart gave me of the
Meeds of the Mass.[l]

[i] Casley's Preface to Cat. of Royal Library, xv. —— [k] Pro-
logue to Canterbury Tales, edition 1542. —— [l] Burnett's Specimens of English Prose Writers, i. 157.

It is, however, in the notices left of the above
monarch that we shall find the most ample record of
the early use of velvet and silk in the bindings of
books. In his Wardrobe Accounts, A.D. 1480, kept by
Piers Courtneys,[m] we have many particulars of the
cost of bindings, materials used, &c.   " To Alice
Claver for the making of xvj laces and xvj tasshels
for the garnysshing of divers of the Kinges bookes,
ij s. viij d; and to Robert Boillett for blac papir and
nailles for closyng and fastenyng of divers cofyns of
fyrre wherein the Kinges books were conveyed and
caried from the Kinges grete Warderobe in London
unto Eltham aforesaid v d. ; Piers Bauduyn stacioner
for bynding, gilding, and dressing of a booke called
Titus Livius xx s. ; for binding, gilding, and dressing
of a booke of the Holy Trinite xvj s. ; for binding,
gilding, and dressing of a booke called Frossard xvj s. ;
for binding, gilding, and dressing of a booke called
the Bible xvj s. ; for binding, gilding, and dressing of
a booke called Le Gouvernement of Kinges and
Princes xvj s. ; for binding and dressing of thre smalle
books of Franche price in grete vj s. viij d. ; for the
dressing of two bookes whereof oon is called La For-
teresse de Foy, and the other called the Book of
Josephus iij s. iiij d.; and for binding, gilding, and dressing of a booke called the Bible Historial xx s."

For the binding of these books another entry is
made of the materials used ; from which it appears

---

that, as in the case of apparel, &c., worn by our kings
and nobles, they procured the materials and employed
workmen to execute the article wanted.   " Delyvered
for the coveryng and garnysshyng vj of the Bookes
of oure saide Lorde the Kynges, that is to say, oon of
the Holy Trinite, oon of Titus Lyvius, oon of the
Gouvernal of Kynges and Princes, a Bible, a Bible
Historialle, and the vj^{the} called Frossard.   Velvet,
vj yerdes cremysy figured; corse of silk, ij yerdes
di' and a naille blue silk weying an unce iij q'
di'; iiij yerdes di' di' quarter blac silk weying iij
unces; laces and tassels of silk, xvj laces; xvj tassels,
weying to gider vj unces and iij q'; botons, xvj of
blue silk and gold; claspes of coper and gilt, iij paire
smalle with roses uppon them; a paire myddelle, ij
paire grete with the Kynges Armes uppon them;
bolions coper and gilt, lxx; nailes gilt, ccc."[a]

And again, " To Alice Claver sylkwoman for an
unce of sowing silk xiv d. ;" for " ij yerds di' and a
naille corse of blue silk, weying an unce iij quarters
di' price the unce ij s viij d. v s. ; for iiij yerds di' of
quarter corse of blac silk weying iij unces price the
unce ij s iiij d. vij s.; for vj unces and iij quarters of
silk to the laces and tassels for garnysshing of diverse
Books price the unce xiiij d. vij s. x d. ob. ; for the
making of xvj laces and xvj tassels made of the
said vj unces and iij quarters of silke price in grete

        a Wardrobe Accounts, &c. 152.

ij s viijd. and for xvj botons of blue silk and gold price in grete iiij s."

"For the copersmythe for iij paire of claspes of cooper and gilt with roses uppon them price of every paire iij s. for two paire of claspes of coper and gilt with the Kings Armes upon them price the pair v s. and for lxx bolyons of coper and gilt xlvj s. viij d."[o]

The "velvet cremysyn figured with white," cost the king viij s per yard.[p] The *bolions* named were a smaller sort of button used as fastenings of books, &c.—made of copper and gilt, and cost about eighteen-pence each.[q] At this time the wages of various workmen were from fourpence to sixpence a day.[r]

By the above account it is evident that the books belonging to the king's library were adorned with all the splendour the best materials, and state of the art could give to their exteriors. Successive monarchs of this country were not less interested in the appearance of their libraries, and velvet continued for some time to be a favourite and the principal cover for at least such works as were considered valuable. In the Privy Purse expenses of Henry VIII.[s] we find the following entries from the year 1530 to 1532. "Paied to Westby clerk of king's closet for vj masse books. And for vellute for to cov[r] them iij l. xj s. To Rasmus one of the Armerars for

[o] Wardrobe Accounts, 117, 119.——[p] Wardrobe Accts Edward IV. 116.——[q] Notes to do. by Nicolas.——[r] Nicolas's Remarks on do ii.——[s] Edited by Nicolas, 8vo. Pickering.

garnisshing of boks and div's necessaryes for the
same by the king's comaundment, xj l. v s. vjj d.　To
Peter Scryvener for bying vellum and other stuf for
the king's books, iiij l.　To the boke-bynder, for
bringing of boks fro hamptonco'te to yorke place,
iiij s. viij. d.　To Asmus the armerer, for the garnisshing of iiij-xx. vj. boks as apperith by his bille. xxxiiij l.
x s.　And paied for sending of certeyne boks to the
king's bokebynder, ij s.

And in an Inventory of the same monarch's Guarde-
robe, &c. made by virtue of a commission under
the great seal of England, dated at Westminster,
September the 14th, 1547,[t] the following notices
occur :—" A Massebooke covered with black velvet,
a lytle booke of parchement with prayers covered with
crymsen velvet.　Also in one deske xxxj bookes
covered with redde ; and in another deske, xvj bookes
covered with redde."

The privy purse expenses of Henry's daughter,[u]
afterwards Queen Mary, also furnish us with further
evidence :—In January 1542—3, " was paied to the
boke bynder for a boke lymmed w^t golde, the
same geuen to the p'nce g'ce for a newyer' gifte,
xxix s.　In the following year, to my ladye Herbert,
a boke cou'ed w^t silv' and gylt, vij s. vj d. ; and in
1537, was paid for a claspe for a boke, vj s."

These accounts prove that a degree of splendour
was lavished on the exterior coating of books almost

[t] MSS. British Museum, No. 1419. A and B.——.[u] Edited
by F. Madden, Esq. F.S.A. 8vo. Pickering.

unknown to our day; for without the cost of what is properly the *binding*, it is seen that Rasmus, or Asmus, who doubtless was the same person, is paid on one occasion, for garnishing of divers books, eleven pounds, five shillings, and seven pence; and on another no less than thirty-four pounds, ten shillings, for garnishing eighty-six books, about eight shillings each for the mere embellishment alone of them, which we take to mean fixing the clasps, bosses, &c. to the sides. The splendour of some of these early bindings may be gathered from the poet laureat' of this period, who, speaking of a book, and enraptured with the appearance of it, breaks out in verse :—

" With that of the boke lozende were the claspes,
   The margin was illumined al with golden railes,
   And bice empictured with grass-oppes and waspes,
   With butterflies, and fresh pecocke tailes,
   Englored with flowres, and slymy snayles,
   Envyved pictures well touched and quickely,
   It would have made a man hole that had be right sickly,
   To behold how it was garnished and bound,
   Encoverde over with golde and tissue fine,
   The claspes and bullions were worth a M pounde,
   With balassis and carbuncles the border did shine,
   With *aurum mosaicum* every other line," &c.

To return, however, it appears also from the extracts before quoted, that there was then such a servant of the court as the KING'S BOOKBINDER. They go far too to clear the eighth Harry from the charge of knowing nothing of, and caring less for fine books. That his predecessor Henry VII. col-

^v Skelton 46.

lected a magnificent library, the various splendid specimens that still exist, bearing his arms on the bindings, is full evidence ; but there can be no doubt it was considerably augmented by his son, under the skilful direction of the great antiquary, Leland, whom Henry had appointed his librarian, and who, in his visit to the various monasteries, must have become possessed of many rare manuscripts and fine books. This is borne out by Heutzner, a German traveller, who, describing the royal library of the kings of England, originally in the old palace at Westminster, but now in the British Museum, which he saw at Whitehall in 1598, says, that it was well furnished with Greek, Latin, Italian, and French books, all *bound in velvet*, of different colours, yet chiefly red, with clasps of gold and silver : and that the covers of some of them were adorned with pearls and precious stones."

Among those originally belonging to Henry VII. is a very curious book of Indentures in the British Museum. It is dated July 10, in the nineteenth year of his reign, and made between him and the abbot and convent of St. Peter's, Westminster, for the celebration of certain masses, &c. to be performed in Henry VII.'s chapel, then intended to be built. It is indeed a most noble and curious book, the cover is of crimson Genoese velvet, edged with crimson silk and gold thread, and with tassels of the

" Warton's Eng. Poetry, iii. 272.

H 2

same material at each corner. The inside is lined
with crimson damask. On each side of the cover are
five bosses, made of silver, wrought and gilt; those
in the middle have the arms and supporters of Henry
VII., with his crown and supporters of silver, gilt and
enamelled; in the others, at each corner, are so many
portcullises, also gilt and enamelled. It is fastened
by two hasps, made of silver, and splendidly enamelled with the red rose of the house of Lancaster.
The counterpart of these indentures, bound and decorated in all respects like the original, is preserved in
the Record Office in the Chapter House, at Westminster.[x]

In the British Museum, also, among the royal
MSS., is the Old Testament, Psalter, Hymns, &c.
(2 B. vii.), formerly belonging to Queen Mary,
bound in a truly regal style It has thick boards
covered with crimson velvet, richly embroidered
with large flowers in coloured silks and gold twist.
It is further embellished with gilt brass bosses and
clasps, on the latter of which are engraved the arms
of England.

Several other specimens of velvet binding are still
in existence in our public libraries. This style continued in use till at least the end of the sixteenth
century: Queen Elizabeth, on her visit to Cambridge,
in 1578, was presented by the vice-chancellor with
"a Newe Testament in Greek, of Robertus Stephanus,

his first printing in folio, bound in redd velvett, and lymed with gould; the armes of England sett upon eche side of the booke, vearey faire." [y]

A custom of perfuming books at this period is shown in the instructions relative to presents to the queen, sent by the Lord Treasurer Burghley to the vice-chancellor of the university on this occasion. He says " Present a book well bound," and charges them " to regard that the book had no savour of spike, which commonly bookbinders did seek to add, to make their books savour well." [z]

Every thing tends to show that Elizabeth was profuse in the embellishment of the bindings of her books; and this doubtless influenced many to present her works in a costume she would be likely to approve. Among the new year's gifts, sent her in the twenty-seventh year of her reign, was a Bible from Absolon, master of the Savoy, bound in cloth of gold, garnished with silver and gilt, with two plates of the royal arms. [a]

Of the labour and expense incurred we have an illustration in the copy of archbishop Parker's " De Antiquitate Ecclesiæ Britannicæ," in the royal library in the British Museum, presented to her by the archbishop. It is a small folio of the date 1572, covered with green velvet. and the front or first side embroidered with coloured silks and silver thread, in

[y] Hartshorne's Book Rarities of Cambridge, 5.———[z] Nichol's Progresses of Elizabeth, ii. 1.———[a] Ibid. Preface, xxvi.

deep relief, as accurately shown in the annexed plate. It is conjectured that the learned churchman intended the design as a reference to his name of Parker. It represents a park inclosed by railings, having in the centre a large rose tree, and deer in various positions. The reverse of the binding has a similar design, but the interior occupied by five deer, one in the centre reposing, the other four like those described, being transposed ; two snakes and various small shrubs are' disposed in the space between. The back is divided into five compartments, by embroidered lines, having a red rose with buds and branches between each, except the second from the head, on which has, at some subsequent period, been placed the title on a piece of leather, thus :

PARKERUS
DE ANT
EC. BRIT.
LOND. 1572.

The bottom one bears on a small piece of leather, fixed on the embroidery—

The book has been rebound in green morocco, but the sides and back as above described, placed over the morocco in a very creditable manner. It is now

Leo sc

FAC-SIMILE

OF THE EMBROIDERED VELVET BINDING OF ARCHBISHOP
PARKER'S DE ANTIQUITATE ECCLESIÆ BRITANNICÆ,

FORMERLY BELONGING TO QUEEN ELIZABETH.

properly preserved in a red basin cover, and further protected by being placed in a box.

Another book of Elizabeth's, also in the British Museum, merits especial notice from its binding. It is the "Historia Ecclesia," printed at Louvain, in 1569, bound in green velvet, with the shield of the royal arms embroidered with coloured silks, and silver and gold thread on crimson silk, in the centre of each side. The remaining spaces are filled up with roses, foliage, &c. formed of the same materials, and some of the flowers composed of small pearls, many of which are lost. The back is similar to the last described, and bears the queen's initials.

Her successor, the first James, appears also to have been partial to a velvet exterior. Specimens may be cited:—among others, the "Panciroli Not Dignit," Lugduni, 1608, in light blue velvet, richly gilt, and having worked gilt edges on a red ground, partly left blank as ornament. But the most splendid specimen, and perhaps the most perfect, of early embroidery on books, is to be found in the British Museum, in the "Acta Synodi Dort," printed at the same place, in 1620, also once the property of James I. No engraving could give a proper idea of its splendour. It is a folio in crimson velvet, the arms of England being embroidered on both sides with gold thread, yellow silk forming the groundwork, but which is entirely hid by the gold, which is embroidered considerably in relief. The initial I surmounted by a crown is worked above, and R similarly below, as

are the rose and thistle in opposite corners.   The
bands on the back are formed with the like material,
and the rose and thistle alternately between each.
It is lettered on leather, the head-bands and gilt
edges neatly executed, and the boards tied together
in front with scarlet riband.   Altogether the workmanship and material are of the first quality, and
constitute it a regal book in every particular.

But velvet was not the only cover for books during
this period; silk and damask were also in general
use for that purpose.   Alexander Barclay, in his
" Ship of Fooles," (1500—1552) speaking of the
company, has the following lines, relative to the
student or bookworm, whom he rather inconsistently
places as the first fool in the vessel :—

" But yet I have them in great reverence,
And honour, saving them from filth and ordure ;
By often brusshing, and much diligence,
Full goodly bounde in pleasaunt coverture
Of damas, sattin, or els of velvet pure :
I keep them sure, fearing least they should be lost,
For in them is the cunning wherein I me boast." [b]

The various extracts above cited, prove that
velvet, silk, or damask were the principal covering
made use of for the best bindings, up to the end of
the fifteenth century, and continued to be partially
used for books belonging to the royal library, a century after.   In addition, it has been shown that they
were lavishly ornamented with all the skill that in-

[b] Warton, iii. 77.

genuity could devise.   Nor did the highest and the
fairest consider it beneath their dignity to exert their
skill in this service, by adding to the covers the embroidered ornament before described.   This is called
Tambour binding, and a Psalter, bound with a large
flower, worked in tambour upon one side of it, is in
the British Museum, which flower is considered, by
Dr. Dibdin,[c] to be the work of Queen Mary.   Be this
conjecture or not, it is certain that ladies at this
period were more conversant with this style of book
ornament than a mere inspection would imply.
Lady Jane Grey, in an exhortation written to her
sister, the night before her execution, thus expresses
herself :—" I have here sent you, my dear sister Ka-
therine, a book, which although it be not outwardly
trimmed with gold, or the curious embroidery of the
artfullest needles, yet inwardly it is more worth than
all the precious mines which the vast world can
boast of," &c. [d]   A copy of this letter in the British
Museum,[e] varies a little from the above :—" I haue
sent yo good sust[r] K. a boke wh although it be not
outwardly rimid with gold," &c.

From this, and the great love of books which Lady
Jane Grey is known to have had, it may be pronounced all but certain that she was accustomed to
employ some of the leisure she possessed in the embroidery of the covers of them.   In the Bodleian

[c] Bibliograp. Decameron, i. 99.——[d] Nicolas's Lady Jane
Grey, 41.——[e] Harl. MSS. 2370.

library, at Oxford, is an English translation of St
Paul's Epistles, in a binding of this description executed by the princess Elizabeth, afterwards queen,
while imprisoned at Woodstock, during the reign of
her sister queen Mary.   The cover is of black silk,
curiously embroidered with mottos and devices
Round the extreme border of the upper side is worked

" CŒLUM PATRIÆ. SCOPUS VITÆ XPVS.
CHRISTO VIVE."

In the centre a *heart*, and about it,

" ELEVA COR SURSUM IBI UBI E. C."*

On the other side

" BEATUS QUI DIVITIAS SCRIPTURÆ LE-
GENS VERBA VERTIT IN OPERA."

And in the centre, round a star,

" VICIT OMNIA PERTINAX VIRTUS E. C."†

A volume of prayers bound in crimson velvet,
among the royal MSS. in the British Museum, claims
the same distinction as the preceding work.   On each
side is embroidered with silver thread a monogram,
apparently composed of the letters R. H. K. N. A. and
E. in high relief, with the letter H. above and below,
and a rose at the four corners.

From what has been previously stated it is evident

Gent's. Mag. New Series, i. 63.

* *Est Christus.*——† *Elizabethæ* Captivæ, or *Elizabetha Captiva.*—
NICHOLS' PROGRESSES, preface.

that Elizabeth was a great lover of books, and a munificent patron of all concerned in their embellishment. But she displayed her taste in this particular further than we have yet shown, by causing the binding to be composed entirely of silver or gold. Of this description is the " Golden Manual of Prayers." It is bound in solid gold, and she is said to have always carried it about with her, hanging by a gold chain. The subject on one of the sides represents the judgment of Solomon, whose sentence appears round the margin ; on the other side is delineated the brazen serpent, with the wounded Israelites looking at it : the motto round the margin is the divine command given to Moses, relative to the making of this serpent. It has been engraved in the Gentleman's Magazine, and Mr. Horne's Introduction to Bibliography. In the inventory of Queen Elizabeth's jewels, plate, &c., made in the sixteenth year of her reign, several ornamental books are also described : amongst others, " Oone Gospell booke, covered with tissue and garnished on th' onside with the crucifix and the Queenes badges of silver guilt, poiz with wodde, leaves, and all, cxij oz." And "Oone booke of the Gospelles plated with silver, and guilt upon bourdes with the image of the crucifix ther upon, and iiij evangelists in iiij places, with two greate claspes of silver and guilt, poiz lii oz. gr. and weing with the bourdes, leaves, and binding, and the covering of red vellat, cxxjx oz."[g]

[g] Archæologia, xiii. 221.

We have been led by the richness of these bindings to a comparatively recent period, and must now
return to the beginning of the fifteenth century, and
to the consideration of two other kinds of early
binding, vellum and calf. We have before stated
that a common forrel was the first cover for books in
the monastic ages of this country. Several specimens
of this description may be met with. The oldest still
preserved is considered by Dr. Dibdin to be a copy of
the "Turrecremata of Alric Han," 1467, the rarest
book in earl Spencer's library, and still in good
preservation. This description of binding was frequently so constructed as to leave a portion of the
forrel or parchment projecting from the boards and
wrapping over the foreedge so as to meet nearly in
the centre of it, and more effectually preserve the book
from injury. Vellum appears to have been introduced
for binding in the early part of the fifteenth century,
but at first was quite plain. At the same period or
earlier, a covering of leather was made use of, but
which species of binding having continued in general
use up to the present time, we shall proceed with the
description of vellum binding first. It cannot be
positively stated in what year vellum began to be
stamped, but we shall not be far wrong in fixing the
introduction of this embellishment about the end of
the fifteenth, or the beginning of the sixteenth century. It is evident the art was known in 1467, as
David Casley, before referred to, describes the bind-

ing of a MS. of the Epistles of St. Jerome, as bearing
the following inscription : — " Liber ligatus erat
Oxonii, in Catstrete, ad instantiam Reuerendi Domini
Thome Wybarun, in sacra theologia Bacalarii Monachi
Roffensis, Anno Domini, 1467.''[h]   This is the earliest
date known to have existed on the cover of a book,
but it unfortunately has been replaced by a modern
binding, and the original lost for ever.

Of these vellum stamped bindings innumerable
specimens exist in various libraries, particularly the
Basil books of the sixteenth century.   Nothing can
exceed the delicacy and beauty of the execution of
some of them, and for sharpness, brilliancy, and proportion, no ornamental decoration of modern days
has yet been introduced that can fairly take precedence
of these works of the binders of early times
Whether the talented artists who executed many of
these were natives or settlers in London, Oxford, or
Cambridge, or of other towns on the continent where
printing had made greater progress, cannot now be
stated, though from what will hereafter be advanced
it is reasonable to suppose many of them were produced in this country, for the race of bookbinders in
1553, was sufficiently numerous in England, and of
such consideration, as to be expressly protected by
an act of parliament against their foreign competi-
tors.   Some of the most costly are impressed with a

---

[h] MSS. Reg. 6. D. II.—See Dibdin's Bib. Dec. ii. 449.——
[i] See Act 25 Henry VIII. 1533.

I

design nearly the full space of the boards ; others are
ornamented with portraits, arms, mottos, or elaborate
devices ; and the year in which the book was bound
was frequently impressed in large figures on its
covers.

When the art of impressing these designs on the
side was first introduced cannot be ascertained. It
will be seen that it had been employed on leather
previously to vellum, but it must have been a work of
some time to bring it to that perfection which we
witness on some early covers. In the absence of
earlier data, the most reasonable conjecture appears
to be that the effects produced by the printing press,
suggested to the minds of the early practisers of that
art, the idea of giving, by means of impression from
wooden blocks, an additional beauty to the side covers
of their books, and that it speedily followed the invention of printing in 1438. But if, by any existing
specimens of binding of this character, it could be
proved to have preceded that era, it might become a
matter of much speculation, how far the result had an
influence in the first essays in block printing by Gut-
tenburg and others.

Specimens of this stamped vellum covering may be
seen in the British Museum, as well as the libraries
of the curious, and among the splendid stocks of the
principal old booksellers of the day ; some executed
with a finish not yet in modern times equalled, and
some bearing a confused mass of ornament too close

to produce any effect.   The portrait of Luther is from

the cover of a book bound in 1569, which bears a
similar one of Calvin on the reverse.   It was in the
possession of Dr. Dibdin, who describes the portraits
as being executed with great spirit and accuracy, and
surrounded with ornamental borders of much taste
and richness.[k]   As this subject will be more fully
discussed under the head of Stamped Leather Bindings, specimens of which are much more numerous,

[k] Bibliomania, 158.

i 2

we shall defer further mention of this style here.
But it may be stated that from a passage in "The
Devil's Law Case," a drama by John Webster, first
published in 1623, it is very evident that gold ornament had been long familiarly known as applied to
vellum binding, at that period.   He says

> " There's in my closet
> A prayer-book that is covered with *gilt vellum*,
> Fetch it."[l]

Of the early use of leather, Montfaucou mentions
several specimens of calf-skin glued boards; and
Robert Copeland, in his poetical prefix to Chaucer's
Assembly of Fools, 1530, says

> " Chaucer is dede, the which this pamphlete wrate
> So ben his heyres in all such besynesse
> And gone is also the famous clerke Lydgate
> And so is youge Hawes, god theye soules addresse
> Many were the volumes that they made more or lesse
> Theyr *bokes* ye lay up tyll that the *lether* moules.[m]

This extract from Copeland proves leather to have
been the common material for the covers of general
works previous to, and in his time.   But a stamped
leather binding on oaken boards, as before referred
to, was, in a period earlier, peculiar in the style of
bookbinding.   Dr. Dibdin has given several engraved
specimens in his Bibliographer's Decameron, and in
citing his description of them, we have pleasure in
acknowledging the handsome manner in which permission has been granted to copy some of the engravings in illustration of the present work.

Webster's Dram. Works, ii. 128. Pickering, 1830.——
     [m] Dibdin's Typ. Antiq. ii. 279.

He first speaks of a copy of the *Spira Livy*, of 1470, in the collection of the Right Honourable Thomas Grenville, as an "extremely perfect and magnificent specimen of this oak-covered leather binding," and of a *Mazarin Bible*, of the supposed date of 1455, in the possession of the late Mr. George Nicol, bookseller to the king, the latter of which " exhibits the central and corner bosses upon the stamped-calf covered boards, into which it was originally put ; possibly under the superintendence of old *Fust* himself." Neither of these, he considers, can be later than the year 1472, but the latter probably full twelve years earlier. An old cover of a MS. of *Claudian* of the thirteenth century, in the British Museum, is a very early specimen of this style. The leather is of a dark colour, having the interior cover of vellum attached to it. The ornaments are displayed with taste and much diversified, being representations of birds, animals, and the human figure, some of them with inscriptions, as

"PAVLVS" "A. GNVSDEI."

" I will now continue" says the Doctor, " the history of this characteristic stamped-calf binding. Portraits or small historical subjects are however rarely seen before the year 1480 : as arabesque were the prevailing ornaments during the fifteenth century. They began pretty early in the sixteenth century with these portraits or small historical subjects. About a dozen years later (1526), as I conceive, is the com-

position of the *Vision of Augustus*, exhibited upon
the same kind of binding. The plate represents the
subject. It was taken from an old cover, like that of
Claudian, which was lent to me by Mr. Buckman,
who had considered it to be an object of some little
curiosity. Do the initials below designate the name
of the artist who achieved this wonderful deed ?"[a]

As it will be found that several of the early printers
usually impressed their *monogram* or *typographical
device* on the sides of their books, we shall not be
hazarding much on the above, in according the initials
and designs at the bottom, to some early professor of
the art, particularly when it is found that even the
names of many were impressed in full, either round
the borders or at the foot, as thus

LVDOVICVS * BLOC * OB * LAVDEM *
XPRISTI* LIBRVM* HVNC* RECTE* LIGAVI

A small folio missal of the latter end of the fifteenth
century, the property of the late Mr. Henry Broadley,
of Ferrily near Hull, presented in the centre of a
stamped calf binding in four compartments the name
of JOHANNES GVILEBERT as the binder. In the collection of the late Mr. Douce, now in the Bodleian
library, Oxford, is a specimen with this inscription :

" JORIS DE GAITERE ME LIGAVIT IN GANDAVO
OMNES SANCTI ANGELI ET ARCHANGELI DEI
ORATE PRO NOBIS."

Another cover bears the name of " JEHAN NORRIS."

[a] Bib. Decameron, ii. 466.

THE VISION OF AUGUSTUS, FROM A
STAMPED CALF BINDING OF THE FIFTEENTH CENTURY.

SIDE COVER OF A STAMPED CALF BINDING
OF THE FIFTEENTH CENTURY.

Initial letters and names in full length may be met with on many of the specimens of early workmanship.   On others inscriptions only, as

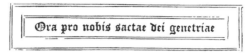

which occurs on the side covers of a work printed at Strasburgh, in 1527 ° But a much earlier specimen is found in the facsimile of the stamped-leather cover of a MS. Biblia Sacra, on vellum, with an illumination of the Madonna and child, from the fine collection of Mr. James Bohn, Bookseller, London.   It is very boldly impressed on the leather, which forms the cover of the MS. without any addition of boards, being simply attached to the back.   The design fills the whole space on the sides.

The Anthologia Græcæ, of 1494, in the Cracherode collection in the British Museum, is a very early specimen of stamped binding,—most probably of the same period, the year being dated on the back.   It is also of a very curious character, presenting some features requiring particular notice. The book is covered with a deep red basin, and to the eye of the unpractised would be taken for an inferior kind of morocco.   This leather is *worked* into a groove formed deep on the edges, so as to

° Dibdin's Bib. Decameron, ii. 468.

present the appearance of a double board.   No ornament is seen on any part except the centre of the
boards, which have been hollowed out in the form of
a circle so as to admit the portraits.   These portraits
consist of cameo heads of Philip and Alexander, the
latter being inscribed.   Whether they were impressed
previous to the cover being fixed, admits of a question ; certain it is they could not have been executed
after covering unless the dies were shaped so as to fit
the cavity formed in the board.   The cameos are
plain ; a gold zig-zag pattern is worked round the
circle of the indentations.   The book has gilt edges,
and worked worsted headbands.   This description of
binding is rare.   Earl Spenser possesses a SIDONIUS
APOLLINARIS, printed at Basil in 1542, in this characteristic cameo binding.   The ornament, in hollow,
represents Pegasus on a rock, with a charioteer
driving two horses towards it, with an inscription of

ΟΡΘΩΣ ΚΑΙ ΜΗ ΛΟΞΙΩΣ.[p]

Of this binding with cameo heads, the side cover of
a PETRARCA OPERA, printed at Basil, two years after
the *Sidonius* last named, is a very elaborate and beautiful specimen.   It is in the British Museum, (3 DL.)
The whole of the ornament is worked in gold, in a
clear, distinct, and superior manner.   The book has
been rebound ; but the sides of the original binding,
which measure thirteen inches by eight, are preserved
and fixed on the modern with much judgment.   The

[p] Dibdin's Bib. Decameron, ii. 469.

Lee. sc

FAC-SIMILE OF A GILT CALF BINDING, A.D. MDXLIV.,
IN THE BRITISH MUSEUM.

illustration displays the subject sufficiently clear to require no further explanation, and with it we close the account of early stamped bindings.

As books became more numerous from the progress the art of printing slowly but steadily made, the degree of labour and expense shown to have been lavished on early bindings, was only adopted for rare specimens of the works of ancient writers, or the books of the noble and wealthy. In the edition of the Philobiblon of Richard of Bury, printed in 1599, the altered condition from their splendour is thus expressed:—" Qui (libri) olium purpura vestiebantur et lysso, nunc in cinere et cilicio recubantes," &c.

Several books in the British Museum, but particularly those once the property of archbishop Cranmer, evidence the truth of the above quotation. The latter are bound in a plain brown calf, with the simple addition of a *mitre*, gilt on the back, in an extremely uneven and careless manner. The frontispiece by Hans Holbein, to Cranmer's Bible, which represents Henry VIII. distributing copies of it to the various estates of the realm, displays the binding of all to be of a humble character with clasps. Many presentation copies would be bound in a superior manner, but this shows that the generality of bindings were at that time without much ornament. Stamped calf bindings gave place to almost as great a variety of styles in calf as are common in the present day ; and some of the superior kind still remain to attest the skill of the artists employed, when the cost necessary

for the execution of good binding, was allowed. A folio
in the library of the late Mr. Heber formerly belonging
to Henry VIII. displayed a great variety of ornament,
with the portrait of the monarch painted in the centre
of each side, all in good keeping and well executed.
A very similar binding remains on a French Bible,
printed at Lyons by Sebastian Honorati, A.D. 1566,
once the property of queen Elizabeth, and now in
the British Museum. By the date, 1567, on the
binding, it appears to have been purposely executed
for her. The book has been rebound, but the whole,
or greater part of the ornament on the sides, ingeniously cut out, and fixed to those of the new cover.
The original binding was in calf, and the outline of
the design strongly impressed, worked with gold, and
coloured with white, scarlet, purple, and green, something like the illuminated bindings of the present day.
The general outline is of a most elaborate nature,
scrolls and ornamental detail being worked in a uniform manner round an oval in the centre, and termi-
nating in elegant corners, &c. The oval in the front,
which measures three inches long, contains a miniature portrait of Elizabeth, with a sceptre, but now
much defaced. Round it, on the *garter*, is impressed
in gilt letters

ELIZABETH. DEI. GRATIA. ANG. FRAN. ET.
HIB. REGINA.

The other side is equally ornamented, but having in
the centre the royal arms, and inscribed round,

POSVI. DEVM. ADIVTOREM. MEVM.

One of the compartments, under the portrait of the queen, is filled up with the following design, worked in gold.

The book is seventeen inches long, and near eleven wide.   The edges are gilt upon red, with minute dotted scroll-work added.

Another book of Elizabeth's, in the British Museum, " Petri Bembi Cardinalis Historiæ Venetiæ, lib. xii.," a folio printed at Venice in 1551, is a curious specimen of binding.   The book has no back, but has been cut like the edges and stabbed through, a piece of gilt paper being pasted over. The boards are fastened to the leaves and project over on all sides, similar to the Ceylonese style, which will be seen further on. The boards are covered with brown calf, and a scroll pattern in gold worked on them.   The inside of the scrolls are stained black, and the gilding is not well executed. In one circle formed on the side is lettered

Dieu

Et   Mon

Droyt

and in a corresponding one lower down, the year in
which it was bound.

M. D. L. II.

In two smaller circles are placed the queen's initials,
thus :—

E—R

surmounted by the crown.

In the British Museum, is also a " Ciceronis Orationes," 2 vols. 12mo. Aldine 1540, in another curious
style of binding of this period.   It is in calf, the ornament painted on the sides with a variety of colours.
This consists of a series of scroll-work, surrounding
a crest of a dog.   The binding is rather clumsy.

These specimens will be sufficient, establishing, as
they do, that the binders of this period had introduced
a variety of styles in the bindings of books, and were
still lavish of ornament.   That they continued so to
do in the reign of James I. there will shortly be occa
sion to show, where some additional facts will also be
produced, in descanting on another material for the
covers of books, adopted at a later date, and from
its quality and durability, ever since preferred for the
best bindings.

Some light is derived relative to the materials used
for covers during the period we have been illustrating,
from a letter of the High Commissioners in Elizabeth's
reign, concerning superstitious books belonging to

All Soul's College, Oxford, in 1567, which are described as—" A Psalter covered with skin ; a prick-
song book covered with a hart's skin ; five other of
paper bound in parchment ; and the Founder's Mass
book in parchment, bound in board."q

The introduction of morocco, as a covering for
books, must be dated at a later period than vellum or
calf, and the merit of its application given to the
binders of the continent, to whose workmanship and
this species of binding we shall, in a subsequent chapter, more particularly devote our attention ; though
some early specimens in this style exist in our libraries, the works of English binders of no mean merit.
One, the celebrated Charter, erroneously attributed
to king Edgar, in the British Museum,r is splendidly
bound in red morocco, and lettered, " CARTA REGIS
EADGARI : MARIUM BRIT. DOMINI." This book is
placed on a green silk cushion in a case lined with
green velvet, and covered with a large plate of glass.

When this book was bound cannot now be ascertained ; but at a much later period than the execution
of the text.   To James I. must be accorded the merit
of introducing morocco as a *general* cover for the
binding of his books. Specimens in velvet belonging
to him have been before described as remaining in
the British Museum. In the same national depository
are several morocco bindings bearing his initials and

q Nichol's Progresses of Queen Eliz. i. 107.——r Harl. MSS.
7513.

K

the royal arms, and such a profusion of gilt ornament as to nearly cover the sides. The "Thevet Hommes Illustres," large folio, Paris, 1584, is in green merocco, the royal arms in the centre, surrounded by scroll and ornamental work. Another, the "Cære-moniaile Episcoporum," folio, Rome, 1600, bears the shield of the royal arms in the centre, and the remaining space completely studded with the rose, thistle, &c. The like ornament is also found on another folio, bearing the initials of Charles I.

But James VI., of Scotland, who, by the death of Elizabeth, became the first of England, had long been a patron of bookbinders. A great lover of literature, like many of his royal predecessors, he transferred to the covers of his books some idea of his estimation of their contents. A document found by Mr. Thomson, of the Record Office, Edinburgh, and published by the Bannatyne Club,* not only gives an account of this monarch's books, but many notices of the sums paid to, and transactions with booksellers, printers, and binders. Our subject relates to the latter, and fortunately many items occur which throw considerable light on the sort of bindings and prices paid in the northern capital about the year 1580.

We have seen that there was the "king's bookbinder" in the time of Henry VIII., and here we have an appointment of John Gibson, under the privy seal, dated at Dalkeith, 29th July, 1581, to the like office under James VI.

* The Library of Mary, Queen of Scots, and James VI. 4to.

" Ane letter maid to Johne Gibsoun bukebinder,
makand him Our Soverane Lordis Buikbinder, and
gevand to him the office thairof for all the dayis of
his lyfetyme, &c. &c. For using and exercing
quhairof his heines gevis grantis and assignis to the
said Johne yeirlie the sowme of tuentie pundis usuall
money of this realme, to be payit to him yierlie."

In the previous year a long account of this John
Gibson's, for work done for the king, presents, among
fifty-nine different books, the following items selected
according to sizes to show the variation in price.

JOHNE GIBSONIS BUIKBINDERS PRECEPT.

Zanthig [Zanchius] de tribus elohim fol. gylt,
   pryce .   .   .   .   .   .   xx s
Harmonia Stanhursti fo. in vellene, pryce . x s
Dictionarium in latino græco et gallico ser-
   mone 4° gylt, pryce   .   .   . xx s
Budæus de contemptu rerum fortuitarum 4° in
   vellene   .   .   .   .   . vj s viij d
Commentaria in Suetonium 8° gylt, pryce . x s
Thesaurus pauperum 8° In vellene   .   . v s
Petronius Arbiter 8° In parchment   .   . iij s
Orationes clarorum virorum 16° gylt, pryce x s

P. YOWNG.   Summa of this compt is
               xvij li. iiij s iiij d.

On the back of this account is an order upon the
treasurer, subscribed by the king, and the abbots
of Dunfermline and Cambuskenneth, as follows :—

REX.

Thesauraire we greit yow weill   IT is our will and we charge yow that ye Incontinent efter the sycht heirof ansuer our louit Johnne gipsoun buikbindar of the sowme of sevintene pundis iiij s iiij d within mentionat   To be thankefullie allowit to yow in your comptis keping this our precept together with the said Johnne his acquittance thairvpoun for your warrand Subscryuit with our hand At Halyrudehous the first day of October 1580.

JAMES R.

R Dunfermline A Cambuskenneth

Here we have also further Gibson's receipt :—

" I Johnne Gibsoun be the tennor heirof grant me to haue ressauit fra Robert coluill of cleishe in name of my lord thesaurar the sowme of sevintene punde iiijs iiijd conforme to yis compt and precept within writtin off ye qlk sowme I hald me weill qtent and payit and discharge him hereof for euir   Be thir p'nte subscyuit with my hand At Edr the xv day of november 1580.

Johnegybsone wt my hand.

Whether Gibson came to England with James cannot be determined, or if any of the specimens we have before described are to be attributed to him must alike remain in doubt.   The sums paid him were for such work as was at the time adopted for the general bindings of the possessors of libraries at that period :

Gylt price referring to a superior binding in leather, perhaps *morocco*, as it is seen that about double the price of that paid for *vellene* is charged. Vellum graced the general class of reading books, and *parchment* afforded a protection for the least valued.

James, on coming to the English throne, continued, and most probably extended his patronage of the art. The specimens described at page 79, show him to have been lavish of ornament, and of his regard for literature an instance may be cited from a speech delivered on the occasion of his visit to the Bodleian Library at Oxford, wherein he stated, " if he were not a king, he would desire to have no other prison, and to be chained together with so many good authors."[t]

The various styles previously described continued to be practised to the end of the seventeenth century by a few, but the general character of bookbinding for some time before and up to the close of that period, had become much depreciated, as there will be occasion to show. The materials adopted by Sir Thomas Bodley were principally leather and vellum, and occasionally velvet, as in the princes' (afterwards Charles I.) books,[u] which he had presented to the library. The statutes which he left, and now in the library, show that where it could be conveniently done, he preferred leather to vellum as a cover for his books.

Hearne's Reliquæ Bodleianæ, 1703.—Introduction. ——
[u] Hearne's Rel. Bodl. 217.

" Statuimus etiam, ut libri in posterum de novo ligandi aut compingendi, sint omnes si commode fieri possit coriacei non membranacei."[v]

The styles and colours he adopted were various. He directs that care be taken in the appointment of "the scholars to transmit the books from the packages, that none be embezzled by reason of the *fine binding* of some of the volumes."[w]   And again, " I pray you continue your purpose for colouring such books as you fancy most."[x]   Others he orders to be *guilded*, and gives directions in almost every letter, relative to some department of binding and ornamenting the books.

During some portion of the period we have been treating, the binders of the universities of Oxford and Cambridge were celebrated for their skill in the art. In the year 1588, we find Dr. James, the first appointed librarian of the Bodleian Library at Oxford, had complained to his patron of the London binding, and Sir Thomas Bodley replying, " Would to God you had signified wherein the abuses of our London binding did consist."[y]   And again, wishing to know for what price " *Dominick* and *Mills*," two Oxford binders, would execute an ordinary volume in folio.[z] He afterwards appears to have employed these or other artists, for in another letter to the librarian, he says, " I pray you put as many to binding of the

---

[v] Appendix Statutorum, 24.——[w] Hearne's Rel. Bodl. 274. ——[x] Ibid. 218.——[y] Ibid. 159. ——[z] Ibid. 185.

books, as you shall think convenient, of which I would
have some dozen of the better paper, to be trimmed
with *guilding* and strings;"[a] and sends, at another
time, " money for their bindings, chainings, plac-
ings,"[b] &c.

The establishment of the Bodleian gave a stimulus
to every thing connected with books in Oxford, which
though in some repute as respected binding, still must
have been limited in extent, as the libraries there
were not previously remarkable for superiority. And
according to Sir Thomas Bodley, Cambridge was less
so, as he remarks after his visit to that university,
" the libraries are meanly stored, and Trinity College
worst of all."[c]

The bindings of Cambridge, however, enjoyed an
equal reputation with Oxford.   A decree of the university several years before (A.D. 1523), provided " that
every bookbinder, bookseller, and stationer, should
stand severally bound to the university in the sum of
£40, and that they should from time to time provide
sufficient store of all manner of books fit and requisite
for the furnishing of students; and that all the books
should be *well bound,* and be sold at all times upon
reasonable prices."[d]   The binders in Cambridge at
this period exercised also the trades of booksellers,
printers, and stationers."[e]   Roger Ascham mentions
one Garrett " our booke-bynder," as being resident
here about the year 1544.[f]

[a] Hearne's Rel Bodl. 342.——[b] Ibid. 363.——[c] Ibid. 195.
——[d] Harl. MSS. 7050.—— [e] Gent.'s Mag. 1781, 409.——
[f] Ascham's Eng. Works, 77.

The universities appear to have kept up the reputation of their bindings during and after the troubled
times of the middle of the seventeenth century. The
opposite fac-simile of the decorative part of the side
covers of a large folio Bible, printed at Cambridge,
by John Field, 1659, and evidently the work of the
same period, displays a degree of taste not often met
with in the general volumes of the time. The cover
is of black basin, the back full gilt, as well as the
squares and edges of the boards. The edges are gilt
in a superior manner, and the binding altogether well
executed. This book is now in the possession of Edward Finch Hatton, Esq., of London. At the commencement of the last century a distinguished binder
of the name of Dawson, resided in Cambridge.[g]

During the period we have been treating of, several
valuable libraries were formed in this country. In the
reign of Henry VI. the library of duke Humphrey
was collected at Oxford. Edward IV. and Henry
VII., by their encouragement of printing, and pur-
chases of works printed on the continent, considerably
promoted the cause of learning in England. The
foundation of the royal library, from which so many
specimens have been produced in illustration of the
previous pages, may justly be attributed to Henry
VIII., enriched as it was by MSS. collected by Leland.[h] And, in conclusion, it may be stated that, from

[g] Hartshorncs' Book Rarities of Cambridge, 18.——[h] Astle's
Writing, xx.

MOROCCO BINDING OF A FOLIO CAMBRIDGE BIBLE,
A. D. 1659.

the invention of printing to the close of the seventeenth century, as in monastic times, the churchmen
and lovers of books exercised not only considerable
influence in the style and mode of binding, but were
also well acquainted with the minute details of its
practice.   Some instances have been cited, and many
other notices fully establish the fact.

Myles Coverdale, in a letter to Thomas lord
Cromwell, relative to his translation of the Bible,
says, A. D. 1538, " As concernyng ye New Testament in English, ye copy whereof yor good lord-
shippe received lately a boke by y^r servant Sebastian
ye coke. I besech y^r L. to consydre ye grenesse
thereof, which (for lack of tyme,) can not as yet be
so apte to be bounde as it should be." [i]   Archbishop
Parker, of whom we have before made mention,
maintained in Lambeth Palace, printers, limners,
woodcutters, and bookbinders,[k] and unquestionably
understood something of their various arts.   But Sir
Thomas Bodley displays a perfect knowledge of every
thing connected with the subject.   In his various
letters to Dr. James, he is continually giving directions relative to the bindings of the books in vellum
and leather ;   ordering them to be rubbed by the
keeper with clean cloths, as a precaution against
mould and worms ; and making provision for a proper supply of bars, locks, hasps, grates, clasps, wire,

[i] Smith's Facsimiles, plate 17.——[k] Gent.'s Mag. N. Series, i.
63.

chains, and gimnios of iron, "belonging to the fastening and rivetting of the books."[1]   Bodley's great contemporary, Sir Robert Cotton, was also, doubtless,
equally well versed in the details of binding.   Sir
Matthew Hale, in bequeathing a collection of MSS.
to the library of Lincoln's Inn, says, "They are fit
to be bound in *leather*, and *chained*, and kept in ar-
chives.   Cosen, bishop of Durham, who will be
more particularly referred to in the next division of
the work, appears to have not been less versed in the
art than those who preceded him.   His directions
are as minute as to the paring of the leather, lettering the books &c., as any professed artist could give,
and his secretary expressly directs that the silver
plates for some of the books should be of proper
thickness, and enters into many other particulars,
which will be detailed in the investigation of some
peculiarities in bindings connected with the period
we have so far investigated.

[1] Hearn's Rel. Bodleianæ. ——[m] Appendix to Report on Public Records.

CHAPTER V.

ENGLISH BINDING AND BINDERS, FROM THE INVEN-
TION OF PRINTING TO THE EIGHTEENTH CENTURY,
IN REFERENCE TO THE STYLES OF WORKMANSHIP,
AND SOME OTHER INCIDENTAL PECULIARITIES.

In tracing the history of English bookbinding, as
more particularly connected with the materials used
and style adopted by the successive races of
bookbinders, other facts illustrative of the art,
during the period embraced in the previous chapter,
have been introduced, but many others remain to be
recorded. We shall, therefore, in now taking a
view of the peculiarities, manner, and execution of
bindings in two periods, viz. the sixteenth and
seventeenth centuries, introduce such records as have
been met with further illustrative of the subject.

The influence of circumstances is seen in the exterior of early printed books and manuscripts, bound
after the invention of printing. Luxury and splendour were studied by the great, and a considerable
degree of elegance by all classes of scholars, which

arose from the limited number of copies printed, and the consequent value of them to the possessors. The folio and the quarto were the usual sizes, which from their breadth afforded ample room for the display of whatever taste the ingenuity of the binder might suggest; and from the specimens which have been given of the embellishment of their side covers, it is evident that they were no mean artists. The multiplication of books, it has been seen, led to a less expensive mode of binding, though still retaining much ornamental beauty. This may be pronounced the style peculiar to the sixteenth century. In the whole of the bindings of this period, a minute care attended every operation required. The workmen, or perhaps the printers, whom it has been shown, were also the binders of their works, appear to have been desirous to thus preserve them to posterity. They are folded with an anxious care for the evenness and integrity of the margins, and it is rare that any transpositions of sheets are found. To guard against this, in the infancy of printing, they had a *Registrum Chartarum*, for the convenience of the binder, of the signatures and first words of the sheets. About 1469—70, alphabetical tables of the first words of each chapter were also introduced as a guide to the binder. The name and place of the inventor of signatures is not known; they appear in an edition of Terence, printed at Milan, in 1470, and were introduced by Caxton in 1480. The Abbé Reve ascribes the discovery to

John Koelhof, at Cologne, in 1472.[a] There is a
solidity about these books, which testifies no little
labour in the beating and pressing of the sheets
when folded. They continued the use of a slip of
parchment round the end-papers, and first and last
sheets of many, to preserve the backs from injury,
and to strengthen the joint. The last leaf is also
strengthened with the addition of other paper, and
in this position the fragments of some printed
works and prints, previously unknown, have been
discovered.

They are sewn on a series of strong slips of white
leather, placed at equal distances from each other, so
as to form the division of the back when covered.
Sometimes, double bands, arranged close together,
are seen, the thread tightly and firmly drawn round
in the sewing.   These double bands are very
distinguishable on the cover, a line being run across
in the small grove between them.   The solidity of
this portion of the bindings of the sixteenth century,
coupled with the formation of the back, is seen in
many books which still remain perfectly firm after the
cover has been worn away, nothing but damp appearing to affect them.

The boards are generally of oak, but planed thinner
than those of the period preceding. Some of them
are beviled off to a fine edge, slanting from the leaves
of the book. The bands or thongs of leather are laced
into the board in a similar manner to the present

[a] Johnson's Typogra hia, i. 6 .

L

mode, but part of the wood cut away to make room
for them.

The edges, which are generally cut very true, are
sometimes plain, but the best works gilt.   The latter
are exceedingly well executed, being, with the exception of a little tarnish, still very perfect, brilliant, and
of a yellow tint, mellowed by age.   Some are also
blind-tooled after the first gilding, giving a very rich
effect.   The headbands are sometimes worked in a
similar manner to those of modern days, sometimes
composed of a round plaited twist, fastened at each
end, and at others of strips of coloured leather worked
one over the other.

The oaken boards are found covered with vellum
and calf.   The covers *appear* to have been stretched
tightly over, the arabesque and ornamental tooling
being executed afterwards.   Manual labour and machinery seem to have jointly assisted in this branch
of the art, it being evident a high degree of pressure,
and quickness of execution, was necessary to give the
peculiar finish and sharpness many of the designs
exhibit.   There is scarcely any end to the variety of
the embellishments; portraits, flowers, mottos, scrolls,
and elaborate designs, are profusely spread over the
sides, with the greatest propriety of style and good
taste ; while the backs are frequently covered with
small ornament of a pleasing character.   The
artists who executed them never lost sight of the
effect of true proportion; and the spirit of all their
ornamenatal decoration is a reflection on the taste of

their successors of the seventeenth century, and even of many sons of the craft of times near the present.

The early printers incorporated their typographical device with the designs on the covers. Richard Pynson caused many pretty devices to be stamped on the covers of the books he printed. And Reynes, who lived in St. Paul's Church Yard about the year 1527, embossed his monogram on the books he bound for himself and others. He introduced this in a large design which he embossed, on the covers of his books, consisting of what are usually called "the arms of Christ." This design is formed of a parallelogram, surrounded by double lines, and borders of scroll and ornamental work, shaped like an arch within, under which is placed a shield, charged with the emblems of Christ's passion, as the cross, inscription, and crown of thorns; the hammer, nails, and pincers; the spears, sponge, and dice; the garment, money, lanthorn, sepulchre, &c. The escutcheon is supported by two unicorns, which stand upon a scroll, bearing the motto,

" REDEMPTORIS MVNDI ARMI,"

in rude Saxon capitals. Above the shield is a rich full-faced black helmet, surrounded by mantling, and surmounted by the pillar, scourges, and cock, as a crest. On each side of the crest are the two shields above mentioned. These religious emblems are found on a great number of Missals, Offices, and Hours of Devotion, both manuscript and printed.[b]

[b] Johnson's Typographia, i. 503.

L 2

The gilding of this period is good, a cleanness and distinctness of ornament being generally found. The titles of the books were not lettered on the backs, such as have them are the additions of a more recent period. The custom was to letter them on the fore-edges of the books with ink, as seen in the engraving, page 116. On others they wrote or printed the name on the sides. Sometimes these titles were covered with horn, as has been before shown, and may be seen in a copy of the Hebrew Pentateuch, in four large folio volumes, in the library of Merton College, Oxford.

A curious specimen of binding of this period is mentioned by Scaliger, as being on a printed Psalter his mother possessed. He says the cover was two inches thick, and in the inside was a kind of cupboard, wherein was a small silver crucifix, and behind it the name of *Berenica Codronia de la Scala.*[c] This kind of binding was not unusual on small books of devotion, containing, like the above, some small subject of adoration, or relic of a saint. Mr. Hansard speaks of a book he had seen with a recess for a relic, and the relic a human toe.[d]

The larger volumes of this period are further protected by the addition of metal clasps, corners, bosses, and bands. The clasps are sometimes attached to strips of strong leather, fastened to the boards with rivets, in which way the catch is also secured, Others are of a more elaborate workmanship and finish, being

[c] Palmer's History of Printing, 96.——[d] Typographia, 105.

jointed to a piece of the same material, firmly rivetted
to the sides.   The boards are further protected by
corners of brass, frequently much ornamented, and
extending a considerable way on the cover.   On others,
a plain piece of brass, wrapping only a small space
over, and others simply protected by brass bands
rivetted to the edges of the boards.   The centres of
the boards often present a large plate or boss of brass,
similar in character to the clasps and corners.

Notices of the earlier use of bosses, clasps, and
corners, have before been given.   Wood's MS., in
the Bodleian library at Oxford, was once very su-
perbly bound and embossed.   Much of its beauty is
now defaced ; but on the bosses at each corner is still
discernible AVE MARIA GRATIA PLENÆ.   The colo-
phon states it to have been finished in 1558.[e] A folio
Bible, printed by Barker, in archbishop Whitgift's
hospital at Croydon, Surrey, given by Abraham Hart-
well, secretary to the archbishop, in 1559, presents
a very good specimen of the bindings of the period.
It has a very curiously ornamented cover, protected
by large brass bosses and clasps.   In the library at
Lambeth Palace, is a characteristic binding of the period, richly covered with gilt ornament, on a copy
of archbishop Parker's edition of the Psalms, 4to.
1570.

To prevent the books being abstracted from their
libraries, the worthies of this period were accustomed

[e] Warton, 136.

to chain them to the shelves. Of this peculiarity an early notice occurs relative to the books left by Richard de Bury, to (Durham) Trinity college, Oxford, in 1345. After the college became possessed of them, they were for many years kept in chests under the custody of several scholars deputed for that purpose, and a library being built in the reign of king Henry IV., these books were put into pews or studies, and chained to them. They continued in this manner till the college was dissolved by Henry VIII., when they were conveyed away, some to Duke Humphrey's library.[f] Leland, (1538) speaking of Wressil Castle, Yorkshire, says, "One thing I likid excedingly yn one of the towers, that was a Study, caullid Paradise; wher was a closet in the midle, of 8 Squares latised aboute, and at the Toppe of every Square was a Desk ledgid to set Bookes on Cofers withyn them, and these semid as yoinid hard to the Toppe of the Closet; and yet by pulling, one or al wold cum downe briste highe in rabettes, and serve for Deskes to lay Bookes on."

In an old account book of St. John's College, Cambridge, is this entry :—

" Anno 1556. For chains for the books in this library, 3s. Anno 1560. For chaining the books in the library, 4s." And among the articles for keeping the Universitie Librarie, Maie 1582—" If any chaine, clasps, rope, or such like decay happen to be, the sayd keeper to signify the same unto the v. chan-

King's Munimenta Antiqua, 152, and Warton.——[g] Itinerary, i. 59.

cellour within three days after he shall spy such
default, to the ende the same may be amended."
That books were frequently chained to desks, we
learn from Wood, who, in speaking of " Foulis's
History of the Plots and Conspiracies of our pretended
Saints the Presbyterians," says, " this book hath
been so pleasing to the royalists, that they have
chained it to desks in public places for the vulgar to
read."

Fox's Book of Martyrs was very generally chained
in the churches ; and long prior to its publication
many other books were in like manner secured.   Sir
Thomas Lyttleton, knight, bequeathed, A. D. 1481,
" to the abbot and convent of Hales-Owen, a boke
wherein is contaigned the Constitutions Provincial
and De Gestis Romanorum, and other treatis therein,
which I wull be laid and bounded with an yron
chayne in some convenient parte within the saide
church, at my costs, so that all preests and others
may se and rede it whenne it pleaseth them." [i]

In the church of Grantham, Lincolnshire, was a
library remarkable for being one of the very few
remaining that had its volumes chained to the
shelves.[k]   The books here are now fast going to decay
from neglect.   There are about two hundred volumes,
principally divinity, in various bindings of calf and
vellum, with wooden boards or strong pasteboard.

[i] Nicolas's Test. Vetusta, i. 367.——[k] Hartshorne's Book
Rarities of Cambridge, 17.

The greater portion have a chain attached, as is seen by the sketch of one of the books in this library; which also displays the early custom before referred to of

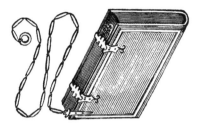

lettering the titles on the fore-edge of the leaves. These books were formerly fixed to strong desks or benches, the ring at the end of the chain being attached to a bolt fastened to the shelves.   It is supposed that this library was first neglected about one hundred and seventy years ago, when, from a great fire that took place in the town, a number of the sufferers were allowed to take refuge in it, until better accommodation could be provided for them; to the great injury of the books, and their total neglect ever after.

This custom of chaining books appears to have been very generally adopted in all public libraries. In the first draft of the statutes Sir Thomas Bodley drew up for his library, he observes, " As it may be lawful and free for all comers in, to peruse any volumes that are chained to the desks, in the body of the library, not forgetting to fasten their clasps and

strings, to untangle their chains,"[1] &c.   He speaks
in one of his letters of their being " chained to prevent embezzlement,"[m] and that they had better be
clasped after they are chained.   His orders for chains
are very frequent and very extensive ; on one occasion for a thousand.   He wishes to know what fault
is found with them, " for I know they will catch, but
yet less than any I have seen," and requests " Mr.
Haidocke to procure clasps for Mr. *Vice Chancellor's*
two great volumes, so that they may be chained, and
stand as a fair ornament."   He also speaks of the
chains being so disposed " that they may not take
away the sight and show of the books ;—of John
Smith, the maker of the chains ;—the chain-
man,"[n] &c.

To the year 1711, at least, did this precaution
against pilfering partially continue.   A paper found
in a copy of " Lock on the Epistles," of this period,
thus enters into the subject.   " Since, to the great
reproach of the nation, and a much greater one of
our holy religion, the thievish disposition of some
that enter into libraries to learn no good there, hath
made it necessary to secure the innocent books, and
even the sacred volumes themselves, with chains—
which are better deserved by those ill persons, who
have too much learning to be hanged, and too little
to be honest, care should be taken hereafter, that as
additions shall be made to this library, of which there

[1] Hearne's Rel. Bodl. 26.——[m] Ibid. 102.——[n] Ibid. 123.
[1]37. 152. 167. &c.

is a hopeful expectation, the chain should neither be
longer, nor more clumsy, than the use of them
requires: and that the loops, whereby they are
fastened to the books, may be rivetted on such a part
of the cover, and so smoothly, as not to gall or raze
the books, while they are removed from or to their
respective places. Till a better may be devised, a
pattern is given in the three volumes of the Centur
Magdeburg, lately given and set up. And foras-
much as the latter, and much more convenient manner of placing books in libraryes, is to turn their backs
outwards, with the titles and other decent ornaments
in gilt-work, which ought not to be hidden, as in this
library, by a contrary position, the beauty of the
fairest volumes is ;—therefore, to prevent this for the
future, and to remedy that which is past, if it shall
be thought worth the pains, this new method of
fixing the chain to the back of the book is recom-
mended, till one more suitable shall be contrived."°

This period had not only introduced great variety
in the styles of binding, but, from the increase in
the number of books, and the consequent greater
employment, a host of craftsmen also ;—so numerous
and important a body, as, in connection with the printers, to have influence enough to obtain the following
Act of Parliament for their protection in the twenty-
fifth year of Henry VIII. (A. D. 1533), which was
not repealed till the twelfth of George II.

° Papers on the Dark Ages, Br. Mag. x. 391.

" Whereas by the provision of a statute made in
the first year of the reign of king Richard III., it
was provided in the same act, that all strangers repairing unto this realm might lawfully bring into
the said realm, printed and written books, to sell at
their liberty and pleasure.   By force of which provision there hath come into this realm, sithen the
making of the same, a marvelous number of printed
books, and daily doth ; and the cause of making of
the same provision seemeth to be, for that there
were but few books and few printers, within this
realm at that time, which could well exercise and
occupy the said science and craft of printing ; never-
theless, sithen the making of the said provision,
many of this realm, being the king's natural subjects,
have given themselves so diligently to learn and exercise the said craft of printing, that at this day there
be within this realm a great number of cunning and
expert in the said science or craft of printing : as
able to exercise the said craft in all points, as any
stranger in any other realm or country.   And fur-
thermore, where there be a great number of the
king's subjects within this realm, which live by the
craft and mystery of binding of books, and that there
be a great multitude well expert in the same, yet all
this notwithstanding there are divers persons, that
bring from beyond the sea great plenty of printed
books, not only in the Latin tongue, but also in our
maternal English tongue, some bound in boards,
some in leather, and some in parchment, and them

sell by retail, whereby many of the king's subjects, being binders of books, and having no other faculty wherewith to get their living, be destitute of work, and like to be undone, except some reformation be herein had.   Be it therefore enacted by the king our sovereigne lord, the lords spiritual and temporal, and the commons in this present parliament assembled, and by authority of the same, that the said proviso, made in the first year of the said king Richard the Third, that from the feast of the nativity of our Lord God next coming, shall be void and of none effect.

" And further, be it enacted by the authority aforesaid, that no persons, resiant, or inhabitant, within this realm, after the said feast of Christmas next coming, shal buy to sell again, any printed books, brought from any parts out of the king's obeysance, ready bound in boards, leather or parchment, upon pain to lose and forfeit for every book bound out of the said king's obeysance, and brought into this realm, and brought by any person or persons within the same to sell again contrary to this act, six shillings and eight pence.

" And be it further enacted, by the authority aforesaid, that no person or persons, inhabitant, or resiant, within this realm, after the said feast of Christmas, shall buy within this realm, of any stranger bourn out of the king's obeysance, other then of denizens, any manner of printed books, brought from any the parts beyond the sea, except only by engross, and not by retail, upon pain of for-

feiture of six shillings and eight pence, for every book
so bought by retail, contrary to the form and effect
of this estatute.   The said forfeitures to be always
levied of the buyers of any such books contrary to
this act, the one half of the said forfeitures to be to
the use of our sovereign lord the king, and the other
moiety to be to the party that will seize, or sue for
the same in any of the king's courts, to be by bill,
plaint, or information, wherein the defendant shall not
be admitted to wage his law, nor no protection, ne
essoin shall be unto him allowed.

" Provided always, and be it enacted by the
authority before said, that if any of the said printers,
or sellers of printed books, inhabited within this
realm, at any time hereafter, happen in such wise to
enhance, or encrease the prices of any such printed
books in sale or binding, at too high and unreason-
able prices, in such wise as complaint be made thereof unto the king's highness, or unto the lord chancellor, lord treasurer, or any of the chief justices of
the one bench or the other, that then the same
lord chancellor, lord treasurer, and two chief justices, or two of any of them, shall have power and
authority to enquire thereof, as well by the oaths of
twelve honest and discreet persons, as otherwise by
due examination by their discression.   And after the
same enhauncing and encreasing of the said prices of
the said books and binding, shall be so found by the
said twelve men, or otherwise, by examination of the
said lord chancellor, lord treasurer and justices, or

M

two of them at the least, that then the same lord
chancellor, lord treasurer, and justices, or two
of them at the least, from time to come, shall
have power and authority to reform and redress such
enhauncing of the prices of printed books from time
to time by their discressions, and to limit prices as
well of the books, as for the binding of them. And
over that, the offender or offenders thereof being
convict by examination of the same lord chancellor,
lord treasurer, or two justices, or two of them, or
otherwise, shall lose and forfeit for every book by
them sold, whereof the price shall be enhanced for
the book, or binding thereof, three-shillings and fourpence, the one half thereof shall be to the king's
highness, and the other half to the parties grieved,
that will complain upon the same, in manner and
form before rehearsed."

That the prices were thus fixed, will appear by the
following extracts, which will also cast some light on
the sums then charged for books and binding. A pro-
clamation of Henry VIII.'s in May, 1540, relative to
Grafton's Bible, then recently printed, sets the price at
ten shillings unbound, and not above twelve shillings
well bound and clasped.[p] At the end of the "Booke
of the Common Prayer," printed by Richard Grafton
in folio, A.D. 1549, is this monition :—"the king's
maiestie by the aduice of his most dere vncle the lord
protector, and other his highnes counsail, straightly
chargeth, and commaundeth that no manner of per-

[p] Lewis's Translations of the Bible, 137.

sone shall sell this present book unbound aboue the price of two shyllynges and two pence. And the same bounde in paste or in bordes in calues lether not aboue the price of four shillynges the pece. God saue the Kyng." Strype relates, that " Sir William Cecil, principal Secretary of State to king Edward, procured for Seres, a printer in St. Paul's Church Yard, in 1569, a licence to print all manner of private prayers, called Primers, as should be agreeable to the Common Prayer, established in the Court of Parliament, and that none other should print the same. And when printed, that by the lords of the Privy Council, or by the lord Chancellor, &c. the reasonable price thereof be set, as well in the leaves, as being bound in paste or board, in like manner as was expressed in the end of the Book of Common Prayer.[q]

It may not be irrelevant here to notice the charge, as we think unjustly, against the early bookbinders, of wanton destruction of many choice and splendid MSS. Portions have frequently been found under the end-papers, on the backs, and even forming the whole of the interior lining or covers of early printed works, which has led to the accusation of the artists of that day having much to answer for on this head. How they became possessed of them has been shown at the period of the Reformation. That the bookbinder's share of the spoil was large is doubtless true, but we may reasonably suppose, that however ex-

[q] Johnson's Typographia, i. 543.

tensive, it did not consist of perfect works; but all more or less mutilated prior to their sale or grant. And even admitting them to have been so, the penalties attached to their diversion from any other purpose than total destruction, would, we apprehend, act upon their minds, and present an effectual bar to the books being even secretly disposed of.

We now proceed to the consideration of the Art in the seventeenth century, and are compelled at the commencement of it to state, that the manner of execution, and style of finish, had altered much for the worse. The old folios of this period possess none of the compactness and beauty observed in the bindings of the previous century. How far this may be attributed to the unsettled state of the country during the civil wars of Charles the First, the stern morality of the Puritans, and the reckless profligacy of the second Charles' reign, cannot for certainty be determined. That these circumstances had much influence cannot be doubted ; for bookbinders, like other artists, lacking the patronage of the wealthy, have not much to stimulate them to greater exertion than the necessity of procuring the means of existence may demand. This state of the art continued throughout the whole of this century. The ponderous volumes of the old nonconformist divines, present little or no variety, being principally covered with an uniform brown calf, without ornamental exterior. Several bindings, however, of this period

ANCIENT BOOKBINDER AND ASSISTANT.

are thickly studded with gilt ornament on the back. Oaken boards had entirely disappeared, and a thick but flimsy pasteboard substituted, the bands, which were of hempen cord being laced in holes pierced through them. A gilt ornament is sometimes seen on the sides : it is of a peculiar character, generally a diamond-shaped tool in the centre, and sometimes smaller ones in each corner. They are badly executed, being dull impressions of an ornament, displaying no taste, and having none of the sharpness of finish necessary to give a good effect.

They continued to beat their books, as in the previous century, in order to produce as much solidity as possible. Of this peculiarity, a poet, Clement Barksdale,[s] has left us the following evidence in his address

"TO THE BOOK-BINDER.

Has my muse made a fault ? Friend, I entreat,
Before you *bind* her up, you would her *beat*.
Though She's not wanton, I can tell
Unlesse you *beat* her, you'l not *bind* her well."

This characteristic of their bindings is also further shown in the annexed engraving of an ancient bookbinder, from an old print; who, though seated and taking his ease more than is now the practice, appears to be hammering away at the book on the stone with a firm determination of doing justice to this depart-

[s] Nympha Libethris, or the Cotswold Muse, 95.

ment. The operation of sewing is also here displayed,
as also in the foliage introduced into the print, the
appearance of the books of the period. The justice
of attention to the sewing and backing of their books
must, however, be given to the craftsmen of this
century, as may be seen in some of the volumes in St.
Paul's Cathedral library, London, which, where preserved from damp, are as firm in this particular as the
day they were executed.

But, in speaking generally, we must not detract
from the merits of a few of the more talented artists
of this degenerated period of our history ; establishing the opinion before expressed, that where patrons
were found, workmen would not be wanting equal to
the task of executing binding in a superior manner.
It is evident that in a few instances a considerable
degree of splendour was bestowed, and vast wealth
expended on the exterior of the books of some of the
lovers of literature. One of these, *bishop Cosin*, not
only lavished great treasure on, but perfectly understood the various manipulations required in the execution of binding. On October 18, 1670, he expressly
enjoins that " the bookes should be all *rubbed once a
fortnight* before the fire to prevent moulding." In
another letter, in the year 1671, to his secretary,
Stapylton, he says, " You spend a greate deale of
time and many letters about Hugh Hutchinson, and
the *armes he is to set upon my bookes*. Where the
backs are *all gilded over*, there must bee of necessity
a piece of *crimson leather* set on to receive the stamp,

and upon all paper and parchment bookes besides.
The like course must be taken with such bookes as
are rude and greasy, and not apt to receive the stamp.
The impression will be taken the better if Hutchinson
shaves the leather thinner."   With such knowledge
of the practice of bookbinding, we cannot be surprised
at the bishops love of luxury in the coverings of the
choicest works, which the following document attests.

To the Right Rev. Ffather in God, John Ld.
Bp. of Durham.

For one booke of Acts bd. in white lether	0	2	6
For binding the Bible and Comon Prayer and double gilding and other trouble in fitting them	3	0	0
Pd. for ruleing the Comon Prayer, . .	0	8	0
The Totall	3	10	6

This, taking into consideration the value of money
at the time, appears to have been the very height of
luxury and extravagance ; but is nothing when com-
pared with the other ornament lavished on the above
Bible and Prayer.

" Receivd the 31 of January, 1662, of the Right
Reverend Father in God, John, Lord Bishop of Durham, by the hands of Myles Stapylton, the summe
of one hundred pounds, being in *part of payment* for
the plate and workmanship of the covers of a Bible
and Common Praier Booke.   I say received by me,
M. S. Houser, Goldsmith, 100*l.*"

This munificent patron of the art does not appear to have confined his endeavours to the embellishment of his own library, and the books of the church over which he presided, but to have influenced by his example the patronage of others.   In a letter bearing the date of Dec. 8, 1662, from Mr. Arden to the bishop's secretary, Myles Stapylton, is this passage. "My Lord desires you to bespeake *black leather cases*, lined with green, for the *silver* and *gilt bookes*, for the countess of Clarendon to carrie and keepe them in." [t]

With support such as this, though the art degenerated so far as the general bindings of the country may be taken into account, a degree of splendour and taste was preserved by a few, which still kept up the remembrance of the talent of previous workmen, with many of their valuable receipts and directions; all which, tended ultimately to the production of a generally improved taste in the eighteenth, and, ultimately, to the perfection of the nineteenth century.   To the consideration of this important result, we shall, in the seventh chapter, devote our attention.

[t] Dibdin's Bib. Dec. ii. 503.

CHAPTER VI.

THE invention of the Art of Printing appears to
have taken place at that happy period, when, from
circumstances, it became of more inestimable value to
posterity by preserving many of the noblest productions of past ages, than perhaps a century later it
would have been possible for it to have achieved.
For, while in its infancy, the fall of Constantinople,
and consequent dispersion of the extensive and magnificent library of the Byzantine emperors, in afford-
ing great facilities to the early printers of the
continent, multiplied the most important classic
treasures, many of which existed in single copies,
and of which the accident of a moment might have
deprived the world for ever. Of the one hundred
and twenty thousand manuscripts which are said to
have disappeared,[a] a valuable portion of them being

---

[a] Gibbon's Rome.

deposited in Italy, thus successively issued from the presses of the early professors of the art, and are preserved to our times by the sturdy integrity and firm workmanship of contemporary bookbinders.

The greater extent of printing on the continent, which rapidly spread to the principal cities of Germany and France, afforded the utmost facility to foreign bookbinders, who consequently increased in number as the commerce in books became extended; and eventually spread themselves over most other countries, many of them permanently settling in England.[b] In commenting on the workmanship of these early settlers, we have, in the previous chapter, also entered into the *detail* of the bindings of the continent also. A repetition of those facts here becomes unnecessary. We shall, therefore, confine our remarks to what is exclusively continental, during the same period.

In the public libraries of the continent, German, French, Italian, Dutch, Spanish, &c. many early specimens of binding. richly studded with gems, or ornamented with silver and gold, still exist, and in the less pretending ones of the monasteries, the oaken boards of the fourteenth century covered with vellum, are found attached to a great number of the books, and still in a good state of preservation.[c]

It is, however, on the continent, as in our own

country, to the patronage of the wealthy and lovers
of books, that we have to attribute the successful
operation of the best workmen.   And in the history
of their libraries, and the specimens remaining, can
we alone trace the progress of the art.   To Corvinus,
king of Hungary, who died, A. D. 1490, must be
assigned the honour of the rank, as first patron of the
period of which we are now treating.   His library consisted of not less than fifty-thousand MSS. and books,[d]
preserved in the most costly bindings, and embellished with all that ingenuity could suggest or
wealth procure.   This splendid collection was preserved in a vaulted gallery.   The books were chiefly
bound in brocade, protected by bosses and clasps of
silver, or other precious metals.   Bonfinius, referring
to them, says, ' cultus librorum luxuriosissimus.'   The
destruction of the library took place in 1526, when
Solyman II. laid siege to Buda. The city was taken by
assault, and the library with all its exquisite appurte-
nances, became a prey to the rapacity of the Turkish
soldiers.   The bindings torn from the books, which
they protected, were stripped of the costly ornaments
with which they were enriched.[e]   Obsopaeus relates,
that a MS. of the Ethiopics of Heliodorus, was
brought to him by an Hungarian soldier, which he
had acquired with many others in the pillage, and
had preserved as a prize, from the cover retaining

[d] Warton's Eng. Poetry, iii. 243——[e] Dibdin's Bib. Dec. ii.
461.

some marks of gold and silver workmanship. Cardinal Bozmanni offered for the redemption of this inestimable collection, two hundred thousand pieces of the imperial money, but without effect.[f] The MSS. were either burnt or torn to pieces, and of the whole collection, scarcely three hundred are now known to exist. Several of these are still preserved in the imperial library of Vienna, but of their original splendour little remains. The public library at Stuttgart, also possesses a MS. St. Austin on the Psalms, covered with leather, and the original ornaments of the time of Corvinus, if not belonging to his library. It is much faded, but the fore edges preserve their former gilt stamped ornaments.[g] There are also in the public library of Brussels, two magnificent MSS. which once graced the library of Corvinus. The first is a Latin Evangelistarium, written in letters of gold upon the most beautiful vellum, and not inaptly called THE GOLDEN BOOK. It had become the property of Philip II. of Spain, who kept it in the Escurial library, under lock and key; and it is said to have been formerly shown to strangers with great ceremony, and by torch light! However this may be, 'tis a precious morceau, and of finished execution.[h] Gibbon awards nearly the same honour to a copy of the Pandects of Justinian, taken at Pisa, in the year 1406, by the Florentines, and still preserved as a relic in the ancient palace of the republic. According to Brenckman, they were *new bound in purple,* deposited in a rich casket, and shown to curious travellers by the monks and magistrates, bare-headed, and with lighted tapers.[i]

While the art thus flourished in Hungary, it was equally successful in Italy, and found in those distinguished patrons of literature, the Medici family, steady supporters, and liberal aid.   The specimens of binding still existing, show that no expense was spared by the Italians of the fifteenth century, in the embellishment of their books.   The manuscripts, &c. collected by Piero de Medici, are highly ornamented with miniatures, gilding, and other decorations, and are distinguished by the *fleur de lis.*   Such as were acquired by Lorenzo, called the father of literature, are also finished with great attention to elegance. They are not only stamped with the Medicean arms, but with a laurel branch, in allusion to his name, and the motto, SEMPER.[k]

To the above liberal patrons of literature, may be added many of the nobles and clergy of Italy, who were profuse in their love of embellishment; but none more so than the celebrated Cardinal Mazarin. His library in his palace on the Quirinal hill, at Rome, consisted of 5000 well selected volumes, " bound by artists *who came express from Paris.*" [l]

[i] Gibbon's Rome, v. 381.——[k] Roscoe's Lorenzo de Medici, ii. 59.——[l] Dibdin's Bib. Dec. ii. 495.

Angelus Roccha, in his Appendix to the Biblia Aposto-
lica Vaticani, 1599, speaking of the library of cardinal
Launcellot, says, it was " celebrated as well on account of the quantity of books, (for there are seven thousand volumes), as for the beautiful binding, their admirable order, and magnificent ornaments." Cardinal Bonelli's library was also celebrated
as being "illustrious for the richest bindings of
books."[m]

There is every reason to believe that a great portion of these bindings, as in the case of the books of
cardinal Mazarin, were executed by workmen of other
countries. The Italians, though furnishing the greater
part of the designs, seen in most ornamental works
of the fifteenth and sixteenth centuries, do not appear
to have ever done much for the art of bookbinding.

The libraries of Germany are particularly rich in
bindings of almost every age and description. Some
specimens have been referred to in a previous chapter,
and others, of which we shall hereafter speak, attest the
patronage bestowed on the art. But though we have
no name, on record, as being, *par excellence*, lovers
of book embellishment, the numerous specimens of
early binding still preserved in Austria, Bavaria,
&c., sufficiently attest a long list of patrons in the
successive rulers of the various kingdoms and states.
In the Imperial library of Vienna, an early specimen
exists on a fine " Evangelistarium." The binding is

<hr>

[m] Dibdin's Bib. Dec. ii. 492.

of the time of Frederick III. (the middle of the fourteenth century.)   The ornaments consist of a lion's
head in the centre of the board, surrounded by golden
rays, and having a lion's head in each corner of the
square.   An arabesque border surrounds the whole,
giving an effect both splendid and tasteful.[n]   Other
specimens might be given to a great extent, both in
this, and the Emperor's private library, in all the
varieties of silver, velvet, silk, calf, and vellum.

A MS. office of the Virgin, in the public library at
Munich, bears witness to the custom of binding books
in silver, with coloured inlaid ornaments, up to the
year 1574, which date it bears.   This library contains also four splendid folio volumes, the text of the
"Seven Penitential Psalms," which exhibit extraordinary proof of the skill of the writer, musician,
painter, and bookbinder.   Of each of these artists,
there is a portrait.   The name of the binder is Gaspar
Ritter.   The books are bound in red morocco, variegated with colours, and secured with clasps.   Every
thing about them is square, firm, and complete, and
stamps Gaspar Ritter as one of the most skilful
artists of the sixteenth century.[o]

In the public libraries of Augsbourg, Stuttgart,
Landshut, &c., similar specimens, clothed in every
variety of material, might be adduced in further
illustration.   In the University library at Leyden,
celebrated throughout Europe, most of the books are

[n] Dibdin's Bib. Tour. iii. 274.—— Ibid.

bound in fine white vellum, and decorated with considerable taste and splendour. [p]

Germany, on the invention of printing, presented
a wide field for the binder; and the artists of that
time do not appear to have neglected the opportunity
presented them.   It is more than probable that they
were also the inventors of the stamped calf and
vellum bindings, which have been fully discussed in
an earlier portion of the work.   That they would not
be slow in applying the knowledge of impression
printing had more particularly brought to notice, may
be inferred, and the covers of many of the volumes
printed in Germany at the commencement of the fifteenth century, by the beautiful stamped devices with
which they are embellished, strongly establishes the
fact. Further than this, the German binding possesses
no peculiarity, and up to the present time, the artists
of that country have never formed what can be called
a national binding.

From the great extent of country, they have, however, always been numerous.   They had at a very
early period laws for their guidance, and the tax, or
price for binding books, in sheep-skin, vellum, &c.,
settled by the magistrates. Throughout the electorate
of Saxony, the prices in sheep were, for large folios,
one guilder or florin, three grosses; common folio,
one florin; large quarto, twelve grosses; common
quarto, eight grosses; large octavo, five grosses;

common octavo, four grosses; duodecimo, three grosses.[q]

These facts, although not presenting us with any particular feature in the history of the art of bookbinding, are interesting as showing the general spread of talented artists at an early period over the several countries of Europe, and that it was very successfully practised during the fifteenth century admits of no doubt. This will be more fully confirmed by the account of French bookbinding, to which we shall now direct our attention.

To the steady and continued support of her kings and wealthy men may be attributed the high position the binders of France for a long period occupied, over those of England or any other country. During the sixteenth century, their superiority was so generally acknowledged that they were sent to most parts of Europe; in the libraries of which, many of their works still remain to prove the judgment of their employers and the skill of the workmen. Of these early French artists, Gascon, Desseuil, Pasdaloup, and Derome, occupy the first rank.

Gascon is considered to have been the workman who bound a considerable part of the libraries of Henry II., and Jean Grolier, of which we shall soon speak, and which will attest the merit of the workman. Desseuil equally excelled in the fineness of his binding, and the elegance of his finishing. Pasdeloup and Derome were contemporaries, and fully bore

---

[q] Fritsch's Dissertation on Bookbinders.

out the reputation of their predecessors. The estimation the bindings of the above artists are held in,
is fully shown by the prices given for many works of
small value from their being coated by them. Of the
latter, may be cited the notice upon Goutard, wherein
the editor explains himself thus, " The books described in this Catalogue are in part bound by the
celebrated Derome, the *phœnix of binders*."[r] And we
may evidence a copy of "Geyler's Navicula Fatuorum,"
sold by auction in London, for 42*l.* from being coated
in a Grolier binding,[s] which book may be bought for
a ducat on the continent.

The royal library at Paris contains innumerable
specimens of the bindings of the period we have above
alluded to. Previous to the reign of Francis I., the
greater portion of the books were covered with velvet,
brocade, &c., of various colours and patterns. Some
still remain, among which, a MS. Ptolemæus, in blue
velvet with a running yellow pattern, now nearly
worn away. Here, also, may be seen many of the
old monastic bindings in ivory, gilt, or brass, studded
with cameos and precious stones, and covered with
figures of all characters and ages.[t] Many of the
books of Francis I. were bound in leather in a plain
manner, differing only according to the tastes of the
countries in which they were bound. With the exception of presents and a few favourite works, all his
Latin, Italian, and French MSS. were bound with

[r] La Reliure, par Lesne, 113.——[s] Dibdin's Bib. Dec. ii. 115.
——[t] Dibdin's Bib. Tour, ii. 59.

black leather.   His Greek manuscripts were partly
bound in the oriental style, and partly in various
coloured moroccos, with smooth backs and no bands.
They are distinguished by the arms of France, and
the insignia of the monarch (a Salamander and the
letter F) stamped in gold or silver. Some of the books
have dolphins added, which indicate the book to have
been bound in the time of Francis, not for the king,
but for the dauphin."

Under the reign of Henry II. it is that we must
look for the celebrated bindings of France in the sixteenth century. The books bound for this prince are
also distinguished by his insignia, or by his initial H,
interwoven with that of his mistress, Diana of Poitiers, HD. We have stated that *Gascon* was the
probable binder of a portion of Henry II.'s books, of
which about eight hundred volumes now remain in
the royal library, bound in a similar manner.   But
the credit of the advances the art made at this period
must be attributed to Jean Grolier, born at Lyons, in
1479, Chevalier, Viscount d'Aguisi, and one of the
four treasurers of France.   This learned and distinguished man was a zealous protector of the arts, and
possessed the most beautiful library, in respect to
size, condition, and binding, at that time known.
Though a kind of leather called morocco had been
in use in the time of Francis I., it is very doubtful
whether the skin dressed as we now see it was applied
as a cover for books previous to its introduction by

u Essai Historique sur la Bibliotheque du Roi, 24.

Grolier. Many of his books exist in the libraries in France and this country, and the estimation in which they are held has been noticed. The beauty, delicacy, and excellent taste of the ornaments are well known and acknowledged. *Vigneul de Malville,*[v] says, "The books were gilt with a delicacy unknown to the binders of his time; he was so much the amateur of good editions, that he possessed all those given by the Alduses, of whom he was the friend : he had them bound in his own house, under his own eyes, and he disdained not at times to put his own hand to them."

Of Grolier's books many are to be found in Mr. Cracherode's collection in the British Museum. They are well and firmly bound. The simplicity of the ornamental work is their great charm. A succession of plain lines forming divers compartments executed with much precision, and attention to proportion, appears nearly on the whole. These designs he is said to have composed himself in moments of leisure when he forsook the more serious cares of his office. They all bear the inscription—

A. J. GROLIER ET AMICORUM,

showing that he wished his books to be used by his friends as well as himself. Of the care his friends took of them, the still perfect state of the bindings amply testifies. Nor must we omit the meed of praise to *Gascon* or whatever other binders he employed,

---

[v] Melanges de Litterature.

SPECIMEN OF THE STYLE OF BINDING OF THE BOOKS
OF THE CHEVALIER GROLIER.

for bindings evidencing a greater care for the integrity of a good margin, and beauty of finish, of no
time or country, are to be met with.   Subjoined is a
specimen of the ornamental side cover of a folio
" Chronicle of Freculphus," 1539, from the collection
of the late Mr. Heber.   It is in brown calf.   The
author's name occupies the centre.

Grolier is considered to be the introducer of lettering pieces between the bands of the back.

How far the taste of Grolier may have influenced,
or whether he had any direction in the binding of
the books of Henry II. to which we must now return, is not satisfactorily determined.   The most
splendid portion of the bindings of Henry, are those
from the fine library at *Anet*, erected by Diana of
Poitiers, distinguished by the interlaced H's and D's.
If not directed by Grolier, she appears to have been
influenced by the splendour of his library ; and with
her unbounded love for books, the wealth she could
bestow, and her influence over the monarch, we need
not wonder at the beauty of the bindings belonging
to her library.   The embellishments are in good
taste, being, like Groliers, principally composed of
lines, interwoven with the initials before referred to,
bows, quivers, arrows, and the crescent, emblems of
the goddess Diana, whose name she bore.

Of the elegance of some of her books, the binding
of a copy of the French version of the " Cosmography
of Sebastian Munster," in the public library at Caen,
in Normandy, remains as evidence.   It is as splendid

as it is curious.   It contains two portraits of Henry
II. and four of Holofernes on each side of the binding.
In the centre of the sides are the usual ornaments
above referred to, but on the back are five portraits
of Diana, in gilt, each within the bands.   Two of
them are faced by portraits of Henry.   There are
also on the sides two pretty medallions of a winged
figure blowing a trumpet, and standing upon a
chariot drawn by four horses, with the date 1553.[w]

It is believed Diana suggested that one copy of
every book to which the royal privilege extended,
should be printed upon vellum and handsomely
bound, as ordered by an edict of Henry II. in 1556.
Of this date the binding of a "MS. L'Historie Ro-
maine," No. 6984, in the royal library, is of extreme
beauty.   The lines in all directions, principally circular, are almost innumerable, and well executed.
The date 1556, is impressed on the outside.[x]

Contemporary with Grolier, another patron, of the
name of Maioli, is well known, from his bindings,
though of his personal history no traces are left.
The decoration of his bindings also consists of designs
in compartments, and bear his name like Grolier's,
thus—

THO MAIOLI AMICORVM.

An Italian edition of the " Psalms of David," 4to.
1534, once belonging to the library of *Maioli*, formerly possessed by Mr. Singer, bears on the reverse
side of the binding the following motto—

[w] Dibdin's Bib: Tour, vol. i. 339——[x] Ibid.

INIMICI. MEI. MEA. MICHI. NON. ME.
MICHI."[y]

The royal library of France exhibits but few bindings of the time of Francis II.   They are marked
with an F. and II.   Some of them have the addition of the initials of Charles IX. from which circumstance it appears likely the books were only partly
finished at the death of Francis.   Those marked with
the cipher Charles IX. are more numerous, impressed
with two C's reversed, and interwoven, sometimes
with K. surmounted by a crown.[z]

Under the reign of Henry IV., the celebrated his-
torian and bibliographer, James Augustus De Thou,
was master of the royal collection.   Under his direction many of the books were bound, principally in red
morocco, and impressed with the royal arms of France,
and the initials of the king.   On some we read the
following inscription—

"HENRICI IIII. PATRIS PATRIÆ VIRTU-
TUM RESTITUTORIS."

as on the MS. Bible of Charles the Bald, which is
highly ornamented with fleur de lis of gold, crowns,
&c.[a]

De Thou also collected a large library of his own,
sparing no expense in procuring copies of the most
celebrated works of the learned.   Jacob[b] says his
library contained more than eight thousand very rare

[y] Dibdin's Bib. Dec. ii. 476.——[z] Horne's Int. i. 299.——
[a] Hist. sur la Bibliotheque du Roi, 35.——[b] Traite de Bibliotheque, 519.

the binding of which, according to Bullialdus, cost
20,000 crowns.   De Thou's favourite colour was red,
principally morocco.   The monogram he adopted was
composed of the initials ADT interwoven.   Others
represent an A between two G's as in the Cracherode
copy of the Libanius of 1606, in the British Museum,
which has on the sides the arms of De Thou and those
of some other person.[c]   This connection of arms appears on several of his books. His bindings in general
are not so ornamented as those of Grolier, but when
they are found, on some of his better books they will
bear comparison with those of that illustrious collector.
Earl Spenser possesses some fine specimens ; and
their estimation by collectors may be gathered from
the sale of "Salvianus on Fishes" for £30 10s, on the
disposal of the late Mr. Edward's library, a book by no
means scarce.[d]   The engraving is from an arabesque
binding of a "Stephens Greek Testament," in the
library of Earl Spencer.

To these distinguished patrons of binding we may
add the names of *Colbert* and *Hoyen*, of *La Valliere*
and *Lainoignon*.   The two great bibliographers of the
time were *Jerome Bignon* and *Gabriel Naude :* the
former, librarian to the king, the other to Cardinal
Onagarius.   The Cardinal's library was next to the
royal collection in extent and magnificence.   Jacob
says it was open every Thursday, from morn till
and curious volumes, all bound in morocco or calf gilt ;

Dibdin's Bib. Decameron ii. 483.——[d] Ibid. ii. 484.

Lee. sc

BINDING OF A STEPHENS' GREEK TESTAMENT,
FROM THE LIBRARY OF THE PRESIDENT DE THOU.

night. In his time there were about 400 MSS. in
folio, bound in virgin morocco and covered with
borders of gold.   The president Longueil could
boast, in Jacob's time, of an admirable collection of
books, which he was increasing every day, and the
library of Nicolas Chevalier formed the basement and
first stories.   "This library," says Jacob, "is one of
the most excellent in Paris for the BINDING, which is
all in calf, covered with fleur de lis, and gilt upon the
edges.   There is also some MSS. very rare, covered
with velvet."   He tells us that in the library of *Claude
d'Urfe*, in the castle of Abbatie, there were more
than 4600 vols. and among which were 200 MSS.
upon vellum, covered with green velvet.   In the
royal library are several works from this collection,
bearing his arms, and splendidly attired.   The library
of the Arsenal also contains some.   Many other
libraries existed.   Guy Patin had 6000 volumes.
The Du Puys about 8000 volumes.   Jacques Ribier
nearly 10,000.   Cardinal Seve had his 6000.   The
duke de la Valliere, a little beyond the middle of the
seventeenth century, had already 20,000 vols.[e] From
the time of Louis XIII. the books in the royal
library ceased to be distinguished by the different
reigns.

In France, as we have shown was the case in this
country, the early printers exercised the art of bookbinding also. Chevallier, in his " History of Printing."
states, that Eustace, Eve, and P. le Noir, each styled

[e] Dil din s Bib Dec. ii. 494.

themselves binders to the university, or the king.
Jean Canivet also styled himself, in the year 1566,
Relegator Universitatis [f]. Louis XIV., by an edict
in 1686, separated the corporation of binders from
the printers of books in the university of Paris; but
by the same edict, the binders were always rated and
reputed of the number of the agents of the university, and enjoyed in this quality the same privileges
they had done before. Two French binders, named
Galliard and Portier, were celebrated for improvements about the end of the sixteenth century.

Were further proof of the distinguished talent of
the early French bookbinders necessary, many other
specimens might be produced. Sufficient has been
done to substantiate this point; but frankly as we
have admitted the superiority of the French bookbinders over all others, during the period we have
been treating of, it will be seen that in the following century they began to retrograde, and their
bindings to possess no distinctive character. They
neglected the illustrious example set before them by
their predecessors, whilst the binders of another
country, profiting by it, bestirred themselves in the
acquisition of the true principles of the art, which,
though progressing slowly for a time, eventually led
to that degree of excellence now exhibited in English
binding, which for some years was not, if now,
equalled, certainly not surpassed, by any other country in the world.

[f] Dibdin's Bib. Dec. ii. 482.

CHAPTER VII.

MODERN BOOKBINDING.

FOR some years no sensible progression or improvement in bookbinding succeeded the period embraced in the three previous chapters of our inquiry. The art, if not retrograding further, still made no advances, and no names, either as patrons or practitioners, in this country or France, occur to redeem the end of the seventeenth and beginning of the eighteenth century from being characterized a dark portion of its history. But a new and brilliant era was about commencing, that was to give a stimulus to the efforts of the English binders, and, by the influence of example, to considerably increase the number of patrons of the art. A taste for the collection and establishment of large and valuable libraries began to develope itself soon after the commencement of the eighteenth century. This materially influenced the sale of books, and incidentally every branch connected with them. New works more frequently appeared, and, from the

o 2

increased demand, in the course of some years, old
ones, that had lain dormant in small collections, or
the secluded libraries of convents on the continent,
were submitted to public competition.   As a consequence, from the greater number of books, binding
began to revive, and by the successive efforts of many
intelligent and talented professors of the art, attained
a perfection in Great Britain, not equalled by the
most splendid efforts of the best days of French bookbinding.

The first and most distinguished of the collectors
of the eighteenth century, was Harley, earl of Oxford, whose fine library, now in the British Museum,
attests his spirit as a collector, and his munificent
patronage of every thing connected with literature.
And when we consider the numerous other patrons of
the book-trade, at this time forming collections, we
need not feel surprise that the eighteenth century,
presenting, as it did, so extensive a field for the talent
and energy of the British bookbinder, was productive
of the most satisfactory results.

The books in the Harleian collection are principally bound in red morocco, presenting but little
variety in the style of finish.   They are what is termed
respectably and soundly bound, with a broad border
of gold round the sides, some with the addition of a
centre ornament ; the fore edges of the leaves are left
plain, and the end-papers are Dutch marble.   The
artist by whom they were bound is not known.

This description furnishes a fair specimen of the

general style of binding till near the close of the
eighteenth century. Materials, of course, differed,
but morocco, russia, and brown calf, were the principal substances. The art may be said to have progressed more in the forwarding, or early stages, than
in the finishing, for it must be confessed, that the selection of their tools for gilding were not often chosen
with the best taste ; birds, trees, ships, &c., being
indiscriminately applied to the backs of books, whose
contents were frequently diametrically opposite to
what the ornament selected would lead any one to
imply. But we must except a few of the bindings of
the period, which evidence better taste. The late Mr.
Hollis had his books decorated in a singular manner.
He employed the celebrated artist Pingo to cut a
number of emblematical devices, as the caduceus
of Mercury, the wand of Æsculapius, the cap of
liberty, owls, &c. With these the backs, and sometimes the sides of his books, were ornamented. When
patriotism animated a work, he adorned it with caps
of liberty, and the pugio or short sword used by the
Roman soldiers ; when wisdom filled the page, the
owl's majestic gravity indicated the contents ; the
caduceus pointed out eloquence ; and the wand of
Æsculapius was the signal for good medicines.[a]

The bindings of Oxford and Cambridge, about a
century ago, continued to be celebrated for their superior workmanship, and are held in high estimation by

[a] Horne's Int. ii. 306.

several modern collectors. The characteristics of the bindings of which we are now speaking, are a peculiar firmness and improved taste of finish. They are in plain calf, with bands, and marbled edges, the spaces between being filled up with gilt tooling.

The middle of the eighteenth century witnessed the introduction of the *sawn back*, whereby the bands on which the book is sewn, were let into the backs of the sheets, and thus no projection appears, as is seen in all bindings of a previous date. Where it was first used is not known, but it is considered the Dutch binding first gave the idea. Although it was adopted by many of the English and French binders with repugnance, it became fashionable. Bands, or raised cords, were soon only used for school books, which species of binding is now universally known as *sheep bands*. The general kind of binding now, up to the end of the eighteenth century, was what is termed *calf gilt*, being done almost all to one pattern, the sides marbled,[b] the backs being brown, with coloured lettering pieces, and full gilt. Open backs had been little introduced, and the backs of the books were made remarkably stiff, to prevent the leather from wrinkling when they were opened.

The artists of the earlier part of the period of which we have been treating must have been numerous, but few are known. Two German binders, of the name of

b On the invention of this process great caution was used to keep it secret, and books were obliged to be sent to the inventor to be marbled at a high price.

Baumgarten and Benedict, were of considerable note, and in extensive employment in London during the early part of this century.[c] Who the distinguished parties at Oxford were has not been recorded, but a person of the name of Dawson, then living at Cambridge, has the reputation of being a clever artist,[d] and may be pronounced as the binder of many of the substantial volumes still possessing the distinctive binding we have before referred to. Baumgarten and Benedict would, doubtless, be employed in every style of binding of their day, but the chief characteristics of their efforts, are good substantial volumes in russia, with marbled edges.

A later artist, and one to whom, perhaps, may be attributed the first impulse given to the improvements which have been introduced into bindings, was Mr. John Mackinlay, one of the largest and most creditable binders in London of the period of which we are now treating. Several specimens of his, in public and private libraries, remain to justify the character given of him ; and of the numerous artists that his office produced, many have, in later days, given good proof that the lessons they received were of a high character.

This century introduced a total change in the aspect of bookbinding, and, by the taste, ingenuity, and efforts of one man, Roger Payne, saw realized all the beauty of the French binding of the times of Grolier and De Thou. This individual, after passing his early

[c] Dibdin's Bib. Decameron, ii.——[d] Hartshorne's Book Rarities of Cambridge, 18.

years at Eton with Pote the bookseller, came to London, and was, some time about the years 1766—70, fixed as a binder near Leicester Square, by the late Mr. Thomas Payne, the eminent bookseller, then living at the Mews Gate. His great taste in the choice of ornaments, and judicious application of them, soon procured him numerous patrons among the noble and wealthy; and had his conduct been equal to his ability, great as were his achievements in the art, it is hazardous to conjecture how much further he might have benefitted it, as well as himself. His books are not so well forwarded as it has been the fortune of the present day to witness. His favourite colour appears to have been olive, which he called *Venetian*. His ornaments were the great boast of his bindings. They were chaste, beautiful, classical, and most correctly executed ; the sides being the field in which he shone most conspicuously. The ornaments of his backs, and his mode of managing bands, were peculiarly his own, and books executed by him are quickly discovered by these characteristic marks. A Glasgow Æschylus, folio, 1795, in earl Spenser's library, which contains many specimens of his binding, is considered to be the *chef d'ouvre* of his workmanship. Of the style and quantity of work employed, the following bill, delivered with it, will show, and also exhibit a curious specimen of his *style*.

" *Aeschylus Glasguae, MDCCXCV Flaxman Illustravit.* Bound in the very best manner, sew'd with strong Silk, every Sheet round every Band, not false Bands; The Back lined with Russia Leather, Cut Exceeding large ; Finished in the most

magnificent manner. Em-border'd with ERMINE expressive of The High Rank of The Noble Patroness of The Designs, The other Parts Finished in the most elegant Taste with small Tool Gold Borders Studded with Gold ; and small Tool Panes of the most exact Work. Measured with the Compasses. It takes a great deal of Time, making out the different Measurements ; preparing the Tools ; and making out New Patterns. The Back Finished in Compartments with parts of Gold studded Work, and open Work to Relieve the Rich close studded Work. All the Tools except Studded points, are obliged to be Workt off plain first—and afterwards the Gold laid on and Worked off again. And this Gold Work requires Double Gold, being on Rough Grain'd Morocco. The Impressions of the Tools must be fitted and cover'd at the bottom with Gold to prevent flaws, and cracks 12 12 0
Fine Drawing Paper for Inlaying The Designs 5s 6d. Finest Pickt Lawn Paper for Interleaving The Designs 1s 6d. | 1 yd & a half of silk 10s 6d. Inlaying the Designs at 8'd each—32 DESIGNS 1. 1. 4. . . . . 1 19 0
Mr. Morton adding Borders to the Drawings   1 16 0

                             £16 7 0

He continued, with varied success, arising from his habits of intemperance, which will be more particularly referred to in the biographical chapter, till the year 1797, on the 20th of November, in which he breathed his last.[e]

Though Roger Payne's career had not been successful, so far as he was personally concerned, it had the effect of benefitting the whole race of English bookbinders. A new stimulus had been given to the trade, and a new and chastened style introduced among the more talented artists of the metropolis. The unmeaning ornaments we have before alluded to

[e] Dibdin's Bib. Decameron, ii. 511.

were discarded, and a series of classical, geometrical, and highly-finished designs adopted. The contemporaries of Roger, Kalthoeber, Staggemier, Walther, Hering, Falkner, &c. exerted themselves with a generous rivalry to execute the most approved bindings, and the efforts of succeeding artists in the persons of Charles Lewis, Clarke, Fairbairn, Smith, &c. have brought the art to the degree of perfection we now see exhibited upon almost every book having any pretension to good binding. The nineteenth century thus witnessed the advance of the art in elegance and elasticity, which no other period previously had developed. Whatever was good in the workmanship of early times was now sought to be revived, and every thing that could be made available, both as regarded variety and superior execution, embraced. Solidity, so much estimated in old bindings, was combined with an elasticity and freedom by means of the open back, which the works of the ancients do not possess. And when to this we add the elegance which modern binding displays, without disparagement to their talent, the palm must be accorded to the modern bookbinder.

A taste, also, for the revival of binding in materials used in the fifteenth and sixteenth centuries soon developed itself. Velvet and silk were reintroduced; the former, from the difficulty experienced in lettering properly, has not been so general as the latter, which is now very extensively adopted for a certain class of books. Modern velvet bindings, however, have been introduced into many libraries, among which may be named the collection of his late Majesty George III., the library of York Minster, earl Spenser, &c.

A style called the Etruscan was also invented by Mr. John Whittaker, and successfully practised by him. This consisted of the execution of designs on the books in tints instead of a series of gold ornament. Castles, churches, tented fields, gothic and arabesque compartments, were executed in their proper colours, and a very unique effect produced. The library of earl Spenser contains a copy of Wynkyn de Worde's " Art and Craft of Living and Dying Well," folio, 1503, bound in this style. The sides are embossed by the device of the printer, projecting to nearly one quarter of an inch. The coat is russia, with a diamond-striped russia leather lining. But the marquis of Bath probably possesses the best specimen of Whittaker's talents as a binder. It consists of a copy of Caxton's " Recuyell of the Historyes of Troye," bound in russia. The back represents a tower, in imitation of stone. On the battlements of it is a flag, upon the folds of which the lettering is introduced, in a character precisely similar to that of the text. On a projection of the tower the name of the printer is impressed. On the outsides of the cover are Trojan and Grecian armour, in relief,

round which is a raised impression of the reeded
axe. The edges of the leaves of this curious volume
are a gold ground, on which are painted various
Grecian devices. On the insides of the covers
(which are likewise russia) is a drawing in India
ink, of Andromache imploring Hector not to go out
to fight ; and on the recto is the death of Hector. [f]

Messrs. Edwards, booksellers of Halifax, in Yorkshire, successfully pursued this branch, and several
bindings of theirs exhibit borders of Greek and
Etruscan vases, executed in a superior manner.

Mr. J. Hering revived stamped calf binding, but
though practised for some time, for the want of a
power of compression, they did not exhibit that
sharpness we see on the impressed bindings of
former times. But this was a step towards the
attainment of the object in view. To our neigh-
bours, the French, must be accorded the merit of
the invention of the modern arabesque, and for its
speedy introduction into, and successful operation in
this country, to Messrs. Remnant and Edmunds, of
Lovel's Court, Paternoster Row, London. The
first specimen executed by them is here faithfully
represented. The extent to which this branch
has in a few years been carried, is almost un-
paralleled; for, from the ease and quickness with
which some of the most extensive designs are produced, the economy is so great, that they have been

[f] Dibdin's Bib. Decameron, ii. 526.

applied to almost every kind of fancy work required in the book trade.

The French also invented a species of illuminated binding, in imitation of some of the interior embellishments of ancient missals. This was for some time kept secret: but one of our enterprising countrymen, Mr. Evans of Berwick Street, Soho, London, after much expense, introduced it into this country. It is a binding of the utmost magnificence, uniting the varied beauties of the arabesque and gilt ornament, with the illuminated decorations of MSS. before the invention of printing. Nothing can exceed the beauty of the whole *coup d'œil*, rivalling as it does the most elaborately finished design of the painter.* From the costly nature of this style of ornament, it must ever be confined to the embellishment of the finest treasures of literature.

Landscapes have also been painted on the sides as well as the edges of books; engraved portraits impressed on, and other designs transferred to, the the sides. Indeed, nothing that could tend to the embellishment and variety of modern bookbinding, appears to have been neglected; and a superiority in the execution of whatever has been attempted is a distinguishing feature of the times.

A peculiarity in a few bindings must not be overlooked. This is, in the coincidence of the cover and the nature of the book. Whittaker bound a copy of "Tuberville on Hunting," in deer-skin, on the cover of which was placed a stag in silver. Jeffery, the book-

* See frontispiece to the *fine edition*.

P

seller, bound Mr. Fox's historical work in *fox's* skin.
And it is related that Dr. Askew had a book
bound in human skin, for the payment of which his
binder prosecuted him.[g]

That the English binders became superior to the
French, is evidenced by the fact of many of the best
bindings of France being executed in London previous to the time of Bozeraine. But at this period
the French binders began to bestir themselves, and
in the productions of the two Bozeraines, Thouvenin,
and Simier, a reputation highly creditable to the
French school is apparent; and the French biblio-
poles have not been backward in claiming an equal
degree of talent and ability for their countrymen
which is accorded to our own.

The nineteenth century, witnessing as it has the
collection of many, and augmentation of other libraries, tended much to this result in both countries.
In England, the art can boast a long list of patrons
in the Dukes of Devonshire, Sutherland, Marlbo-
rough, and Buccleuch, the Marquises of Lansdowne
and Bath, Earls Spenser, Cawdor, Clare, and Burling-
ton, Lords Vernon and Acheson, the Honourable
Thomas Grenville, Sir F. Freeling, Sir R. Colt Hoare,
bart., Sir Mark Sykes, Baron Bolland, Mr. Heber, Dr.
Dibdin, Mr. Hibbert, Mr. Dent, Mr. Bernal, Mr.
Drury, Mr. Petit, and a host of others, who have contributed much to the successful progress of the art.

The increased employment is shown by the num-

g Dibdin's Bib. Decameron, ii. 451.

Morris & Cº Ludgate Stᵗ

MODERN BOOKBINDING.

ber of master binders in London, A.D. 1812. At a
general meeting in December of that year, no less
than one hundred and fifty-nine subscribed their
names to the regulations of prices, &c. adopted. Of
these many were first-rate artists, and several still
continue to execute bindings in the first style of the
art. Doubtless, some are foremost in their profession; but where so many now excel, it would be
invidious to particularize, were it not from a desire
to prevent the names of those who are now eminent
as binders, sinking into that entire oblivion, so far
as the public are concerned, which it has been frequently our lot to deplore, during the investigation
of the subject of the present work. Without passing any judgment on their respective merits, or
peculiarities of workmanship, we shall therefore,
in addition to those before introduced, simply record,
as the leading London bookbinders of the present
day, the names of Adlard, Bird, Burn, Clarke, Fairbairn, Hering, Heydey, Leightons, Lidden, Mac-
farlane, Mackenzie, Smith, Westley, Wickwar, and
Wright. The modern binders of France are Cour-
teval, Lefebre, the Bozeraines, Thouvenin, Simier,
Lemoinier, Basin, Lesne, Matifa, Berthe, Coty, Du-
rand, Bisonare, &c.

The successful operation of some of the processes
we have before referred to, may be attributable to
the great improvements in machinery used in the
art, produced of late years. The hydraulic press,
the rolling machine, and the arming or embossing

press, have done much for the rapid progress of the work, and its more perfect execution. The study of the antique in the ornaments used for finishing, and the superior engraving of the tools, became general. And with the ability to execute, on the part of the workman, a taste for the exterior decoration of books rapidly spread throughout the country. To what greater perfection bookbinding may come it would be hazardous to give an opinion, seeing that now it appears scarcely capable of progressing much further. In the elasticity solidity, freedom, proportion of binding, and style of finish, it has not in any previous time been equalled, and the British binders generally of the present day may be pronounced, without egotism, as the first in their profession. The patronage and encouragement the art has received from all quarters has tended to cause a generous emulation among the modern sons of the craft, and with the most happy results ; for bookbinding has fully participated in the advantages which these favourable circumstances have imparted.

MODERN BOOKBINDING.

CHAPTER VIII.

FOREIGN BINDINGS POSSESSING PECULIARITIES NOT
BEFORE DESCRIBED.

THE advance made by a nation in civilization, the facilities offered for the cultivation of literature, and the natural productions of, or readiness with which substances whereon to write could be obtained, must have ever had a very powerful effect on the modes adopted to preserve the written documents of various countries. Throughout Europe, as has been shown, a great similarity in the manner now exists, however great may be the difference in the beauty of appearance, and the style of finish. This being the case, the few peculiarities that are still found in European bindings will alone require description.

THE FRENCH,

have a style which they call *Indorsing*. Its peculiarity consists in a slip of parchment being applied over the back, between each band, the projecting ends being pasted inside of each board.   It is done in the press, where the back being grated to make the paste take hold, the parchment is fixed, and glue added to further strengthen the back.

THE ITALIANS,

possess a feature peculiar to their bindings, which they call *binding alla rustica.*   It is merely covering the book with a coarse thick paper, and if wished a degree neater, applying a cover of fancy paper over. This proceeding, from the speedy destruction of the paper, is of very great inconvenience.

THE DUTCH,

whose bindings may be classed as the most elastic and solid, generally use slips of parchment, instead of packthread, for the sewing of their books.

THE GERMANS.

A peculiar feature in the German bindings, has acquired some celebrity from its preservation of the large margins, so sought after by the Bibliographer. It is called, *a la Bradel.*   The sheets are cut to the same size before sewing, either single with the shears, or together in the cutting press.   When sewed and boarded, the book is headbanded, and the head, tail, and covers covered with parchment.   The

back is afterwards covered with leather, like a half-
bound book, or wholly with fancy paper; most commonly, the latter. This style has been executed in
France, and a volume, the first done in Paris, was
presented to Charles X., in a beautiful binding of this
description. It was entirely covered with gold paper,
the edges gilt, the sides and back richly ornamented,
and the letters of the title executed in silver. The
binding was from the hands of *M. Berthe*, senior,
No. 10, Rue Hautefeuille, Paris.[a]

The bindings differing totally in appearance to
those before described, are the Eastern, and may
be classed under three heads: the Indian, the Chinese,
and the Turkish.

THE INDIAN.

The Indian books are usually written on the leaves
of plants or trees, generally the *palmyra*, on which
the letters are engraved with a stylus. The Sloane
library contains several of these MSS. written on
leaves in the Sanscrit, Burman, Peguan, Ceylonese,
and other languages.[b] The Ceylonese appear to
prefer the leaf of the *Talipot* tree, on account of its
superior breadth and thickness. From these leaves
they cut out slips from a foot to a foot and a half
long, and about two inches broad. These slips being
smoothed, and all excrescences pared off with the

[a] La Relieur, par Le Normand, 213.——[b] Ayscough's
Catalogue, 904, 906.

knife, they are ready for use without any other preparation. After the characters have been formed on
the leaf, they rub them over with a preparation of oil
and charcoal, which not only renders them more
distinct, but so permanent, that they can never be
effaced. When one slip is insufficient to contain the
whole of a subject, the Ceylonese string several together by passing a piece of twine through them, and
attach them to a board, similar to our manner of
filing newspapers.[c] But a greater regard for their
preservation is shown for their more extended performances, or for such works as are held in estimation by them, as is displayed in the annexed sketch
of a CEYLONESE BOOK.

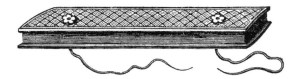

The leaves are laid one over the other. They are
not sewed as in European bindings, but kept together
by two strings, as before referred to. These are laced
through two holes made in each of the leaves,
which are fastened to the upper covering of the book
by two knobs, formed of some expensive article,
sometimes of crystal. The boards which confine the

[c] Percival's Ceylon, 205.

leaves together, are made of hard wood, generally the jack tree, and are often beautifully ornamented and painted.

The Birmans and Hindoos form and compose their books in the same manner, and of like material.[d] A writer in the Asiatic Researches,[e] says, the Burmans, in their more elegant books, write on sheets of ivory, or on very fine white palmyra leaves : the ivory is stained black, and the margins are ornamented with gilding, while the characters are enamelled or gilt. On the palmyra leaves the characters are in general of black enamel, and the leaves and margin painted with flowers in various bright colours. They are bound as before described. In the finer binding the boards are lacquered, the edges of the leaves cut smooth and gilt, and the title written on the upper board. The more elegant books are in general wrapped up in silk cloth, and bound round by a garter, in which the natives ingeniously contrive to weave the title of the book.

The East India Company's library contains a very elegant Burman MSS. in the Pali, or sacred character, presented by colonel Clifford. It is covered with coloured paper, with grotesque coloured figures. Another specimen has the edges partly gilt. This library also contains a very curious specimen of Batta writing, the production of, and presented by, a cannibal chief, Munto Panei. It is bound with plain wood

d Symes's Embassy to Ava, ii. 409.—e Vol. iv. 306.

covers. There is also another covered with leather,
dressed with the hair on.

THE CHINESE.

The Chinese first made use of bamboo, cut very
thin, for the formation of their books, afterwards silk
or cotton. From these they subsequently manufactured paper, of which latter material their paper is
still generally made. From the fineness of its texture,
only one side can be written or printed on.[f] This
circumstance causes a distinct characteristic in the
binding of the Chinese. Two pages are printed upon
one leaf, usually from the top to the bottom, as, seen
in the engraving. The paper is then folded, and sewn
up in the open part, while the close side composes
the outer margin. The blank half of the leaf being
thus joined, the printed part only is visible, which,
from the thinness of the paper, appears as if on opposite sides of a single leaf. The cover is not glued to
the leaves; it is a case wrapped round them, in some
parts double, and secured by a fastening of silk and
bone. When this is loosened, and the boards un-
folded, there appears within from four to six or seven
slightly stitched *livraisons*, about the size of one of our
magazines, which can be taken out and replaced at
pleasure.[g] The cover or case of the Chinese bindings,

f Morrison's Miscellany, 33, 34.——g Astley's Collection,
iv. 162-3.

here represented, is formed of a brown pasteboard, made of a species of smooth and strong
paper. For their common books an addition of
a cover of fancy paper is adopted; but for those in
greater repute, they employ silk, or a species of
taffeta with flowers, which they use almost solely for
this purpose. Some of their books are covered with red
brocade, ornamented with flowers of gold and silver.
The title, written or printed on a slip of paper, is
generally pasted upon a corner of a cover. Several
of these Chinese books may be seen in the library of
the East India Company.

THE TURKISH.

The early sovereigns of Turkey established *Kitab
Khanès*, or public libraries, in the great cities of their
empire. In Constantinople alone, there are now
thirty-five, containing from one to five thousand
manuscripts each. The followers of Mahomet have

a peculiar mode of binding their books. It resembles
that of Europe in the manner of sewing and head-
banding, but the back is left flat, instead of being
rounded, as we are accustomed to form it. The
books are usually covered with red, green, or black
morocco, one of the sides being lengthened out, so
as to fold over the fore edge, and fasten on the
other side like the flap of a portfolio, of which the
engraving will give a just idea.

Sometimes this projection is lodged between the
board and leaves. The covers are enriched with
ornaments, in gold and silver, or blank, as in our
own country. The title of the book is marked upon
the edges of the leaves, and also on the edge of the
outer covering. This covering is a case of similar
material to the binding, in which the latter is placed,
to protect it from dust and injury. The books in the
Turkish libraries, are placed in cases with glass or
wire-work fronts, resting on their sides, one above
another.

CHAPTER IX.

SKETCHES AND BIOGRAPHICAL NOTICES OF BINDERS, AMATEUR PROFESSORS, AND OTHERS, CONNECTED WITH THE ART.

To trace, with anything like distinctness, the lives of many distinguished professors of the Bibliopegistic art, is a task that cannot be accomplished, many being known only by the talent and skill of their workmanship. Connected only with their works, their names passed among their friends and contemporaries, as so distinguished, but with them sunk into oblivion, without other note or record. Though during life, thus keeping the even tenor of their way, there are many reasons for placing on record in this work what is known of such persons, who, from living in early times, or distinguished for superior talent in modern, command a degree of interest beyond those of less notoriety. The most important, perhaps, is the stimulus to those of the present, and coming days, to look forward to the like approbation

Q

of, and success in, the world, which a diligent attention may, and will certainly lead to.   And warned by the failures and errors of others, to avoid the temptations they are liable to be led into, and eventually forfeit a character for talent and integrity, no otherways to be obtained.   But not less important is the record of their names with the History of the Art, with which their work, or their endeavours to effect improvements in its various branches, are connected, embodying, as the narrative must do, many facts, and notices not possible to introduce in the previous chapters.   Alike interesting become the few particulars known of such amateur professors, as have devoted their time and study towards the acquisition of a knowledge of the Art, for to the patronage of many, and the assistance of others, it owes a debt of gratitude, for benefits conferred, which in a record of its History, it is but due to acknowledge.

The earliest professors of the Art, whose names have come down to us, are what may be distinguished as

MONASTIC BINDERS,

and those known are but few in number, when we consider that in every abbey, possessing the smallest library, means were always in requisition for the increasing of their MSS., and properly binding them under their own roofs.

DAGÆUS,

an Irish monk of the early part of the sixth century, is the earliest practitioner known, connected with the Art of binding books. He is celebrated as a skilful illuminator of their interiors, and not less so of the embellishment of their exteriors, binding and ornamenting the covers with gold, silver, and precious stones.[a]

BILFRID,

a monk of the abbey of Durham, who lived about A. D. 720, is the first binder in England whose name has reached our time. He is stated to have pre-eminently excelled in the binding and ornamenting of books,[b] and as being " aurificii arte præcipuus." [c] Of his skill and workmanship, a record has been preserved in the binding of the MSS. in the British Museum, described at page 46 of this work.

HERMAN,

bishop of Salisbury, about the year 1080, according to the Monasticon Anglicanum,[d] was well versed in the binding of books, as well as the writing and illuminating of them.

---

[a] O'Conor's Rerum Hibernicarum, clxxvii ——[b] Warton's Eng. Poetry, i. cxliv. dissertation 2.——[c] Simeon Dunhelm, Hist. Eccl. Dunhelm. 117.——[d] Vol. iii. 275.

HENRY,

a monk of the Benedictine abbey of Hyde, near
Winchester, is celebrated for his skill in the binding
of books.   A copy of Terence, Boetius, &c. which he
had transcribed, is stated not only to have been
bound by him, but that he also formed the brazen
bosses of the covers with his own hands.[e]

BINDERS AFTER THE INVENTION OF
PRINTING.

Of the numerous artists that sprung into notoriety
after the invention of printing, little has been recorded, and of many of them, whether resident of
England, it is not known with certainty.   When
printing was in its infancy, many English merchants
found it to their account to import books from the
continent, which, from their scarcity here, readily
found purchasers.   These, as was the custom at that
time, were bound previous to leaving the printer,
who had executed under his own roof, every department, from the casting of the letter, to the binding of
the complete volume.   Two of the names are known
to be foreign artists, and some of the others which
we shall have to record, though existing on bindings
in this country, may belong to the artists of another.

[e] Warton, i. cxliv.

CORNELIUS,

the bookbinder, as he is called in the evidence brought forward in proof of Lawrence Coster, of Haarlem, being the inventor of printing, appears to have been an assistant of Coster, in his youth.[f] He lived there in the year 1440, and doubtless was an artist of some practice and talent at that period.

PIERS BAUDUYN,

Stationer and Bookbinder, appears to have been much employed by Edward IV. in binding and ornamenting the books for his library.[g] The silk tassels, clasps, and other ornament, were previously prepared by the *silkwoman, coppersmith,* &c. and the binding executed by Bauduyn, who perhaps may have been appointed the king's bookbinder, as it will be seen such an office existed in another reign.

RASMUS, OR ASMUS,

living in 1531, and 1532, in which years he was paid considerable sums for the embellishment of the books, belonging to Henry VIII.[h] He is described as being the armourer, but from the loose manner in which accounts were kept, it is not unlikely but that he was the party who not only ornamented, but

[f] Johnson's Typographia, i. 6.——[g] Wardrobe's Account of Edward IV. 125-6.——[h] Privy Purse Expenses of Henry VIII. 123, &c.

bound the books too. In the same accounts, mention is made of the king's *bokebynder*, but whether this applies to Rasmus cannot now be ascertained.

NOWEL.

A bookbinder who dwelt in Shoe Lane, Fleet Street ; was most probably a small binder for the printers of the day in which he lived, about A. D. 1530. It is almost certain, that he was latterly wholly employed by Wynkyn de Worde, and with satisfaction, as we find that he left Nowel in his will, dated June 5, 1534, twenty shillings in books.[a]

ALARD.

The name of this early binder is known only through the will of Wynkyn de Worde, above referred to, as " to Alard, *bookbinder*, my servant, six pounds, fifteen shillings, and fourpence."[b]

L. BLOC.

This is one of four bibliopegistic heroes whose names have been perpetuated by the goodness of their bindings,—or the care the possessors have bestowed on them. Of their personal history, or the locality of their daily labours, nothing is known We can, therefore, do no more than record their names as they have been met with. Bloc's exists

---

[a] Ames' Typographical Antiquities, i. 120.——[b] Ibid.

round the border of a stamped calf cover, of the
latter end of the fifteenth century, thus :—

LUDOVICVS BLOC OB LAVDEM XPRISTI LIBRVM HVNC
RECTE LIGAVI.[c]

JOHN GUILEBERT.

Is known only from a similar impression on a
small folio of the same period, where he is desig-
nated as " JOHANNES GVILEBERT." The style of
binding and ornament of these two latter persons
appear much alike.

J. DE GAITERE.

Conjectured to be of Ghent, in Belgium, from the
inscription, which is introduced at page 90, ante.

J. NORRIS,

The last of the above referred to, impressed his
name, " *Jehan Norris,*" on the books he bound.
The whole of these persons must have been men
celebrated in their day, and probably contemporaries.
The sums necessary to be disbursed for the designs
on the books, whereon their names appear, could not
have been the case had they not been men of some
note in their profession ; and though positively nothing can be pronounced, still it is not an unfair
presumption to consider them as first-rate artists of
the times in which they flourished.

c Dibdin's Bib. Decameron, ii. 467.

JOHN REYNES.

This person was an eminent Bookseller and Binder, residing at the George in St. Paul's Church-yard, about A.D. 1527. Many books of this period have his marks and devices impressed on their covers, as he bound many books for other dealers beside himself. His devices were two small shields, with his initials and his monogram. These he usually introduced in a large design, which he embossed on the covers of his books. It is not known in what year he died, but it is supposed about 1544. The Stationers' company formerly possessed a portrait of him.[d]

MICHAEL LOBLEY,

one of the original members of the Stationers' company, united the branches of Bookseller, Printer, and Bookbinder, at the St. Michael, in St. Paul's church-yard. He filled several offices in the Stationers' company, but in the latter part of his life appears to have been so much reduced, as not to have been able to discharge his note for 7*l.* which he stood indebted to the company; for having paid 3*l.* " the rest was forgiven him by the hole table." [e] He carried on business from A.D. 1531, to 1563.

JOHN TOYE.

Little further is known of this person, than his being engaged with John Day, the celebrated printer,

<hr />

[d] Ames' Typog. Antiq. i. 120. ——[e] Ibid ii. 756.

a pursuivant and other officers, by order of the bench of bishops, in search for a work called, "The Puritanic Admonition to the Parliament," wherein the government of the English church was attacked with great severity. This was about 1566. It is more than probable that this is the same person, as the John Toye, living at the sign of St. Nicholas, in St. Paul's church-yard, which appears on a " Gradus comparationum cum verbis," &c. 4to. printed in 1531.[f]

WILLIAM HILL.

Originally a printer, who lived at the sign of the Hill, in St. Paul's church yard. The books bearing his name are dated 1548 and 1549. He is considered to have left off printing, and devoted his attention to bookbinding. He was fined in 1556, for binding primers in parchment, contrary to the Company's orders.[g]

JOHN GIBSON,

Bookbinder to James VI. of Scotland, being appointed to that office in the year 1581. He appears to have been an artist of some celebrity, as seen in the account of his work, and other particulars referred to, at page 99. Gibson had been employed by James, previous to his appointment, as shown by the following entries in the accounts of the High Treasurer of Scotland :—

[f] Ames, i. 56 ——[g] Ibid. ii. 756.

Maii 1580.

Item be the Kingis Majesteis precept to Johnne Gibsoun buikbinder, for certane buikis furnist to his hienes, conforme to his particular compt, as the samyn with the said precept and his acquittance schewin upoun compt beris,   xlj lib. vj s.

October 1580.

Item be the Kingis Majesteis precept to Johnne Gibsoune buikbindar, ffor certane buikis maid be him to his hienes, conforme to the particular compt gevin in therupoun, as the samin with the said precept and his acquittance schewin upoun compt beiris,   xx li.

Januare 1582.

Item be his Majesties precept to Johnne Gibsoun buikbindare, for sindrie volumes bund to his hienes, as the precept with his acquittance producit upoun compt beris,   v lj. xvj s. viij d.

Marche 1582.

Item for binding of the New Testament to his Majestie be Johne Gibsoun buikbindare,   xiiij s.[h]

ANDREW HART.

A Scotch bookbinder in the time of James VI., of whom nothing is known except his having bound some books for the above monarch. In the accounts above referred to is the following entry:—

[h] The Library of Mary Queen of Scots, and James VI. 4to.

Aprile 1602.

Item payit to Andro Hart Buik binder, for certane buikis quhilkis wer gevin to Mr Adam Newtoun for the Prince his use, as the said Mr Adamis ressait thairof producit testifeis,   xxxj li. ix s.

GARRET.

a bookbinder at Cambridge, about 1544. The binders here at that period were considered superior workmen, but of the personal history of this man, nothing is known. Roger Ascham, speaking of Erasmus' custom of riding on horseback for exercise, after "he had been sore at his booke," says, "as Garrett, *our booke-bynder*, verye oft told me. [k]

DOMINICK AND MILLS.

Two Oxford binders of good reputation about the year 1597 ; and considered by the Oxonians of that period superior to those of London.   In answer to a complaint from Dr. James, the first keeper of the Bodleian library, we find Sir Thomas Bodley writing, " I am sorry to hear of those abuses of my binder. Send me word at what price your binders will bind an ordinary book in folio."   And again, " would to God you had signified wherein the imperfections of our London binding did consist."[l] He also promises,

[k] Ascham's English Works, 77.——[l] Hearne's Relquae Bodleianæ, 159 and 185.

if the Oxford price " is reasonable, I will send sufficient work for *Dominick* and *Mills*, or some other for a month or two."

MODERN BOOKBINDERS.

In proceeding to give a few notices of the modern sons of the craft, the name that claims priority, as being the greatest binder England had, up to his day, produced, is that of

ROGER PAYNE.

The personal history of Roger Payne is one, among the many, of the ability of a man being rendered nearly useless by the dissoluteness of his habits. He stands an example to the young, of mere talent, unattended with perseverance and industry, never leading to distinction,—of great ability, clouded by intemperance and consequent indiscretion, causing the world only to regret how much may have been lost, that might have been developed, had the individual's course been different, and his excellences directed so as to have produced the best results.

Roger Payne was a native of Windsor Forest, and first became initiated in the rudiments of the art he afterwards became so distinguished a professor of, under the auspices of Mr. Pote, bookseller to Eton college. From this place he came to London, where he was first employed by Mr Thomas Osborne, the

ROGER PAYNE.

bookseller, of Holborn, London. Disagreeing on
some matters, he subsequently obtained employment
from Mr. Thomas Payne, of the King's Mews, St.
Martin's, who ever after proved a friend to him. Mr.
Payne established him in business near Leicester-
square, about the year 1766-1770, and the encouragement he received from his patron, and many wealthy
possessors of libraries, was such that the happiest
results, and a long career of prosperity, might have
been anticipated. His talents as an artist, particularly in the finishing department, were of the first
order, and such as, up to his time, had not been developed by any other of his countrymen. He adopted
a style peculiarly his own, uniting a classical taste in
the formation of his designs, and much judgment in
the selection of such ornament as was applicable to
the nature of the work it was to embellish. Many of
these he made himself of iron, and some are yet
preserved as curiosities, and specimens of the skill of
the man. To this occupation he may have been at
times driven, from lack of money to procure them
from the tool-cutters ; but it cannot be set down as
being generally so, for in the formation of the
designs in which he so much excelled, it is but
reasonable to suppose, arguing upon the practice of
some others in later times, he found it readier and
more expedient to manufacture certain lines, curves,
&c. on the occasion. Be this as it may, he succeeded
in executing binding in so superior a manner as
to have no rival, and to command the admiration of

the most fastidious book-lover of his time. He had full employment from the noble and wealthy, and the estimation his bindings are still held in, is a sufficient proof of the satisfaction he gave his employers. His best work has before been described, as being in earl Spenser's library. The following bill relates to an ancient edition of Petrarch in the same collection.

The paper was very weak, especialy at ye Back of this Book. I was obliged to use new paper in ye Washing to keep the Book from being torn or broken. To paper for Washing,................	2	0
To Washing their was a great deal of Writing Ink and the bad stains, it required several washings to make the paper of the Book quite safe, for, tho the Book with one or two washings would look as well at present, it will not stand the test of Time without repeated washings. Carefully and quite Honestly done,.............................	9	0
To Sise-ing very carefuly and Strong,........	7	6
To Sise to Sise the Book, ...	1	6
To mending every Leaf in the Book, for every Leaf wanted if thro' the whole Book, especialy in ye Back Margins. I have sett down ye number of pieces to each Leaf,*......................	10	6
Cleaning the whole Book,..................	4	0
	1 14	6
The Book had been very badly folded and the Leaves very much out of square ; I was obliged to Compass every leaf single, and mark the irregular parts, and take them off without parting the sise of the Copy, very carefully, and Honestly done,......	3	6
The Book being all Single Leaves, I was obliged to stich it with silk fine and white, to prepare it for sewing done in the Best manner and uncommon,	2	6

The copy of the Book was in very bad Condition when I received it. The most Antiq. Edition I think I have ever seen. I have done the very best; I spared no time to make as good and fair a

* At foot of the bill is an enumeration of the pieces.

Copy as is in my power to do for any Book, that
EVER DID, or EVER WILL, or EVER CAN be done by
another workman ; thinking it a very fine unique
edition. Bound in the very best manner in Venetian
Coloured morocco leather, sewed with silk, the
Back lined with a Russia Leather. Finished in the
Antiq. Taste, very Correctly lettered, and very
fine small Tool Work, neat Morocco joints, Fine
Drawing Paper inside to suite the colour of the
Original paper of the Book. The Outside Finished
in a True Scientific ornamental ¦Taste magnificent.
The Book finished in the Antiq. Taste, very cor-
rectly letter'd in Work. The Whole finished in the
very Best manner for preservation and elegant
Taste, ... 4   7   0

Here we have the whole minutia of the mode of
proceeding, and this appears to have been a peculiarity in all his bills, each book of his binding
being accompanied by a written description of the
ornaments in a like precise and curious style. Here
is another relative to a book bound for Dr. Moseley;
which also exhibits a little jealousy of his brethren of
the craft, or a due appreciation of his own talent, by
the contemptuous manner he refers to them.

Versalii Humani Corporis fabrica. The title Washed, Cleaned
and very neatly Mended, The opposite Leaf Ditto. The *Por-
trate* Margins Cleaned and the opposite Leaf Ditto. Fine
Drawing Paper inside, exceedingly neat and strong mo-
rocco joints. Fine purple paper inside very neat. The Outsides
Finished with Double Panes and Corner Tools *agreable* to the
Book. The Back finished in a very elegant manner with small
Tools, the Boards required *Peice-ing* with Strong Boards and
strong Glue to prevent future Damage to the Corners of the
Book. 2 Cutts new Guarded. The former Book-binder had
mended it very badly as *usial*. I have done the very Best
Work in my Power according to Orders, took up a great deal of
Time.   0*l*. 15*s*. 0*d*.
In another Bill he says, 'The Back coverd with Russia

R 2

Leather, before the outside cover was put on. N.B. The
Common practice of Book-binders is to line their Books with
Brown or Cartridge Paper, the paper Lining splits and parts
from the Backs and will not last for Time and much reading.

These are only a few of the curious and characteristic specimens of the bills of our artist, but they are
sufficient to attest the superiority of his workmanship
over the living binders of the day, and the justness of
its appreciation by the most distinguished bibliopo-
lists. But his reputation as an artist of the greatest
merit, was obscured, and eventually nearly lost, by
his intemperate habits. He loved drink better than
meat. Of this propensity an anecdote is related of a
memorandum of money spent by, and kept by himself, which run thus :—

      For Bacon, - 1 half-penny,
      For Liquor, - 1 shilling.

No wonder then, with habits like these, that the efforts
of his patron, in fixing him, were rendered of no avail.
Instead of rising to that station his great talent would
have led to, he fell by his dissolute conduct to the
lowest depth of misery and wretchedness. Of his
squallid appearance, an idea may be formed by the
annexed engraving. It is taken from a print, which
Mr. Payne caused to be executed after his death, at
his own expense, and exhibits the man in his
wretched working-room, as in life he daily appeared.
Here, however, was executed the splendid specimens
of binding we have before referred to ; and here on
the same shelf were mixed together old shoes and

precious leaves—bread and cheese, with the most valuable and costly of MSS., or early printed books.

That he was characteristic or eccentric may be judged by what has been related of him. He appears to have also been a poet on the subject of his unfortunate propensity, as the following extract from a copy of verses, sent with a bill to Mr. Evans, for binding " Barry on the Wines of the Ancients," proves.

> " Homer the bard, who sung in highest strains
> The festive gift, a goblet, for his pains ;
> Falernian gave Horace, Virgil fire,
> And Barley Wine my British Muse inspire.
> Barley Wine, first from Egypt's learned shore ;
> And this the gift to me of Calvert's *store*."

He commenced business in partnership with his brother Thomas Payne, and subsequently was in like manner connected with one Richard Wier, but did not long agree with either, so that separation speedily took place. He afterwards worked under the roof of Mr. Mackinlay, but his later efforts showed that he had lost much of that ability he had been so largely endowed with. Pressed down with poverty and disease, he breathed his last in Duke's Court, St. Martin's Lane, on the 20th of November, 1797. His remains were interred in the burying-ground of St. Martin's in the Fields, at the expense of Mr. Thos. Payne, who, as before stated, had been his early friend, and who, for the last eight years of his life had rendered him a regular pecuniary assistance both for the support of his body and the performance of his work.[a]

Of the excellencies and defects of his bindings, a party well qualified to judge, and to whose researches we are indebted for greater part of this memoir, has thus recorded his opinion, and with which we shall close our account :—

" The great merit of Roger Payne lay in his taste —in his choice of ornaments, and especially in the working of them. It is impossible to excel him in these two particulars. His favourite colour was that of *olive*, which he called *Venetian*. In his lining, joints, and inside ornaments, our hero generally, and sometimes melancholily failed. He was fond of what he called purple paper, the colour of which was as violent as its texture was coarse. It was liable also to change and become spotty; and as a harmonizing colour with olive, it was odiously discordant. The joints of his books were generally *disjointed*, uneven, carelessly tooled, and having a very unfinished appearance. His backs are boasted of for their firmness. His work excellently forwarded—every sheet fairly and *bona fide* stitched into the back, which was afterwards usually coated in russia; but his minor volumes did not open well in consequence. He was too fond of thin boards; which in folios produces an uncomfortable effect, from fear of their being inadequate to sustain the weight of the envelope.[b]

[a] Nichols's Literary Anecdotes, iii. 736.——[b] Dibdin's Bib. Dec. ii. 508.

RICHARD WIER.

A partner of Roger Payne's, and one not a whit less dissolute than himself. Previous to this, he and his wife,* viz. in 1774, were employed at Toulouse, in binding and repairing the books in count Macarthy's library. The connexion between Wier and Roger, which took place during the latter part of Payne's career, as might be expected from both of their habits, was of short duration. They were generally quarrelling, and Wier, being a man of strong muscular power, used sometimes to proceed to thrashing his less powerful coadjutor. Payne is said to have composed a sort of *Memoir of the Civil War* between them. After their separation, Wier went abroad; and being taken prisoner by a privateer, he is said to have threatened to demolish half the crew if they did not liberate him. Like his partner, he worked the latter part of his life with Mr. Mackinlay.[c]

BAUMGARTEN,

was a German binder of some note in London, in the early part of the eighteenth century, but of whose personal history nothing has been left on record.

[c] Dibdin's Bib. Decameron ii. 567.

* Mrs. WIER, celebrated as the most complete book-restorer that ever lived. She was for a long time employed by Roger Payne; and her skill in mending defective leaves was such, that, unless held up to the light, the renovation was imperceptible. On her return from France, she went to Edinburgh to repair the books in the Record Office in that city.

BENEDICT.

Contemporary with Baumgarten, but alike situated, having no other record left of his life and labours than has been recorded at the one hundred and fifty-second page of this work.

JOHN MACKINLAY,

for many years one of the most substantial and creditable binders of the British metropolis. His bindings in general are not so much celebrated for their splendour as for the general goodness of the workmanship. But he sometimes appears lavish of ornament, of which specimens exist in earl Spenser's and other libraries.

He has the credit of being the instructor of many of the most celebrated binders that have since his day sprung into notoriety.

Mr. M., during his latter years, was unfortunate in having his office destroyed by fire.

KALTHŒBER.

A reputable binder of the same period as Mackinlay. He was noted for his russia bindings, and latterly worked in the premises of Mr. Otridge, the bookseller.

STAGGEMIER,

in business at the same period as the above, was a binder of reputation and taste. The Royal Institution possessed the best specimen of Staggemier's skill, in the binding of the " Didot Horace," of 1799, presented by Mr. Thomas Hope. It is in blue morocco, and embellished with ornaments cut after the antique models.

WALTHER,

a binder bearing the character of executing his work in a " good, substantial, honest manner." He had no pretensions for any style peculiar to himself, but gained the character bestowed upon him from the excellent manner every part was performed. In his office the celebrated Charles Lewis gained the first rudiments of the art he afterwards so much excelled in.

HENRY FALKNER,

Celebrated as a honest, industrious, and excellent bookbinder, who, in his mode of rebinding ancient books, was not only scrupulously particular in the preservation of that important part of a volume, the margin : but in his ornaments of tooling, was at once tasteful and exact.[d] Faulkner, after thus giving satisfaction to his patrons, and biddnig fair to be the first binder of his day, died of a consumption in 1812, leaving a large family, which, it is but justice to state, were materially assisted by those who had employed and respected their father.

CHARLES HERING.

After the death of Roger Payne, Hering, for about twelve years, was considered the head of the craft.

[d] Dibdin's Bibliomania, 264.

He was an extremely skilful binder, and a remarkably industrious man. His bindings exhibit a strength and squareness, with a good style of finish, which renders his work of much value, and establishes the reputation accorded to him. His faults were a too great fondness for double headbands, and the use of brown paper linings, with a little inclination to the German taste. Possessing the reputation he did, the principal libraries of this country contain many of his bindings. The business is still conducted by his brother with success.

JOHN WHITTAKER,

was celebrated as the restorer of deficient portions of works printed by Caxton, &c. by the use of brass type; and the inventor of gold printing, now become nearly general. He introduced a new style of binding, to which the name of *Etruscan* has been given. This style he employed for the binding of many of the copies of the Magna Charta, printed by himself in gold. The description of this mode of binding has been given in a previous chapter, and many specimens of other works exist in the libraries of the wealthy and curious. The binding of the copy of Magna Charta belonging to his late Majesty George IV,, is of a magnificent description. The covers are nearly a complete mass of gold ornament, appropriate to the times of king John. It is lined with crimson silk, richly gilt.

CHARLES LEWIS,

one of the most eminent binders the British capital
has produced, and by several considered as being the
first in his day, was born in London in the year
1786; and at the age of fourteen became apprentice
to Mr. Walther, of whom we have given a brief
record.   After serving the full period of his appren-
ticeship, and working as a journeyman in several
shops in the metropolis, he commenced business on
his own account in Scotland Yard. At this place, and
subsequently in Denmark Court, Strand, and Duke
Street, Picadilly, he displayed as much perseverance
and attention in the management of his business, as
skill and energy in the pursuit of the art, he
appears from his first introduction to it at Mr.
Walther's to have been passionately devoted to. His
bindings are to be found in nearly all the libraries of
the modern patrons of the book trade we have before
enumerated, for some of whom he worked very
extensively, and to the satisfaction of his employers.
On the character of his binding, Dr. Dibdin has thus
enlarged :—" The particular talent of Lewis consists
in uniting the taste of Roger Payne with a freedom of
forwarding and squareness of finishing peculiarly his
own.   His books appear to move on silken hinges.
His joints are beautifully squared, and wrought upon
with studded gold ; and in his inside decorations he
stands without a compeer. Neither loaf-sugar paper,
nor brown, nor pink, nor poppy-coloured paper are

therein discovered : but a subdued orange, or buff, harmonizing with russia; a slate or French grey, harmonizing with morocco ; or an antique or deep crimson tint, harmonizing with sprightly calf : these are the surfaces, or ground colours, to accord picturesquely, with which Charles Lewis brings his leather and tooling into play ! To particularize would be endless ; but I cannot help just noticing, that, in his *orange* and *Venetian* moroccos, from the sturdy folio to the pliant duodecimo—to say nothing of his management of what he is pleased facetiously to call binding *à la mode Francaise*, he has struck out a line, or fashion, or style, not only exclusively his own, as an English artist, but, modelled upon the ornaments of the Grolier and De Thou volumes, infinitely beyond what has yet been achieved in the same bibliopegist department. It is due to state, that in his book restorations he equals even the union of skill in Roger Payne and Mrs. Weir.　We may say—

'And what was *Roger* once, is *Lewis* now.' " [e]

After a very successful career, and in the enjoyment of an extended business, he was seized with apoplexy in the month of December, 1835, from which he never recovered, expiring on the eighth day of January, 1836.　His eldest son now carries on the business.

[e] Dibdin's Bib. Dec . ii.

FRENCH BOOKBINDERS.

The reputation of the binders of France, as we have before stated, at one time far exceeded that of any other country. The names of the principal operators, therefore, claim a distinguished place in this chapter. And it will not be irrevelant here to introduce a brief notice of the principal binders of the French capital of the present day.

GASCON.

This person is considered to be the first who introduced an elaborate style of gilt and other ornament on books into France. He lived in the time of Henry II., and is conjectured to have bound part of that monarch's library, as well as that of the chevalier Grolier, who doubtless contributed much to their proper execution by the taste and knowledge of the subject he possessed.

DU SUEIL

threw more of solidity into his work than his predecessor Gascon, while he did not neglect the finish given to his volumes. His reputation stands high among the lovers of books for the goodness of his work, as is attested by the remarks in book catalogues, where any of his bindings are named. A very fine collection of the *Abbé's* handy works were contained in the collection of the count of Brienne,

which was to be sold very cheap at James Wood-
man's and David Lyon's shop, in Russell Street,
Covent Garden, on Tuesday, the 28th day of April,
1724. This library was as select (it had been chiefly
collected by the famous Father Simon, the best
critic in books in his time) as it was magnificent;
the advertisement telling us that " several hundred
of the books had been new covered in morocco by
Monsieur L'Abbe Du Sueil." Accordingly, we read
perpetually " cerio turcico compactem per Abbatem
de Sueil;" or " relie en maroquin per l'Abbe du
Sueil;" or "bound by A. de S., gilt, and marbled
on the leaves;" or " nicely covered in morocco by
the A. du S." Pope, in the fourth epistle of his
" Moral Essays," has contributed to the popularity
of the *Abbé du Sueil.* He was fond of a variety of
colours on his morocco covers, and worked solidly
and elegantly in the taste of his day.

PASDALOUP

was also celebrated for the strength and beauty of
his workmanship. He was fond of red morocco
covers and linings, with a fillet or border of gold
upon each. He sometimes formed his fly-leaf of
gold paper. His work is also often cited in sale
catalogues, and, like the above, will perhaps be so
for many years, as the substantial manner in which
it is executed appears to be capable of lasting for
centuries.

DE ROME.

This person has been styled the *Phœnix* of Binders. He was a contemporary of Pasdaloup, and appears to have worked much in the same style, throwing great solidity into the forwarding of his books, and much elegance into the finishing. His bindings, consequently, are as much sought after, and as highly prized by the possessors.

DE LORME.

A good binder of the same period as Pasdeloup and De Rome, but not so celebrated. His country-men charge him with the imitation of some of the *bad* English binding .

COURTEVAL,

an artist of modern times, presented a new feature in his bindings by the union of elasticity and solidity, now so much and rightly estimated. He appears to have been a man of talent as well as taste, in estimat-ing and adopting the improvements of other nations, and rejecting their errors along with those of his own. Very few workmen of his day united in an equal degree the grace, solidity, elegance, and proportion, that is found in the bindings that came from his hands. Very little, if any, fault can be found in them.

LEFEBRE,

another binder of modern times, who, rejecting the prejudices of custom, adopted the improvements introduced, and, by increased success, justified the expectations he may have formed. His bindings possess no other peculiarity.

BOZERAINE, SEN.

The elder Bozeraine may be said to have reintroduced the good taste of former days into France. He studied the style of his celebrated countrymen of the fifteenth century, and adopted all the judicious improvements that had been introduced elsewhere, carrying it towards that success his brother afterwards accomplished. By his efforts, many distinguished collectors ceased to have their books bound in England; where, from the low state to which the art had sunk in France, they had for some time previous been accustomed to send their best binding

BOZERAINE, JUN.

The younger Bozeraine was considered the first bookbinder in France, and his work consequently held in great repute by the Parisian collectors. He appears to have been ardently attached to his art, and pursued it progressively to the successful issue of being, by his own countrymen at least, considered the first artist in the world. He is said to have been a long time in overcoming the prejudices of many workmen; but he possessed courage to persevere in his endeavours, and finally triumph. It is saying much for his reputation, independent of his workmanship, that his contemporaries admit, nearly all the good workmen have come from his establishment. No wonder, then, that the biblical Parisians make a grand crack about him, and place him in rivalry with Charles Lewis. English book-collectors, however, have not accorded that degree of celebrity to Bozeraine, which his countrymen have freely and lavishly done. His bindings are well known in London. They are considered to be forwarded too expeditiously, and beaten too much. His love of finery, of satinizing, of red ruling, and of gorgeous and flimsy ornament, do not accord with the idea of true propriety and chasteness here so distinguishable on the best bindings.

THOUVENIN.

Unlike Bozeraine, jun. Thouvenin became celebrated as an artist on his first establishment, and his first performances are as much valued as any of his subsequent efforts. Being a pupil of Bozeraine's, he had availed himself of all the good lessons of that distinguished workman, who, as it has been seen, had opened a way for the introduction of the style of binding so much renowned in former centuries. Thouvenin thus had the advantage of being known to all the principal book-collectors, who, on his establish · ment, entrusted him with many of their rare books, and they were not mistaken in their ideas of his talent and ability. He imitated the English gildings, and

s 3

produced several specimens of a Gothic character. In all his work he reflected an honour on his teacher, Bozeraine. He unquestionably was a binder of celebrity ; but whether deserving of the following highly-coloured encomium of one of his contemporaries may admit of a doubt :—

" Thouvenin is one of those extraordinary men, who, similar to that luminous body, a comet, appear but once in a century. If more ambitious of glory than of fortune, he continues to watch ; if less workman than artist, he occupies himself without intermission in the perfection of binding; it will be an epoch in his art, as distinguished as those of the great men that we have admired in the epoch of literature."[f]

SIMIER,

another modern artist, and *relier du roi*, as the backs of some of his bindings testify. He, like some of the above, contributed to the introduction of a better style and taste into France. His bindings, some of which are in this country, are very creditable performances.

LESNE,

a Parisian artist of not much note in his business, but as having written a poem, in six cantos, on the Art of Bookbinding, which he published in 1820.

[f] La Relieure, par Lesne ; 117

This he dedicated to his son. He appears to be enthusiastic on his subject, and handles it with much spirit and cleverness. He suggested some improvements in the manner of sewing books, which should give to them greater freedom, elasticity, and solidity; and in furtherance of his object, presented a " Memoire" to the *Societé d'Encouragement*, in 1818, which met with a favourable report.

Subsequently, in consequence of some remarks on the Parisian binders, made by Dr. Dibdin, in his Bibliographical Tour, Lesne again figured in a pamphlet in reply, taking up the matter for his bibliopegistic brethren, in rather hastier temper than the occasion demanded or warranted.

AMATEUR PROFESSORS.

The number of noble and distinguished persons who have occupied their leisure in the pursuit of the art of bookbinding, is doubtless considerable; but the record of their acts, and the proof of their workmanship, have alike been lost or overlooked. We have referred to some who possessed considerable knowledge of the various processes necessary in binding a book. The account of the Ferrars family, the Hon. Roger North, and the celebrated William Hutton, furnish us with more important details.

THE FERRARS FAMILY.

This family lived at Little Gedding, in the county of Hertford, in the reigns of James I. and Charles I.

200 BIOGRAPHICAL NOTICES OF BINDERS, &c.

They were distinguished for their piety and industry. The greater part of the family, male and female, appear to have understood and practised the art of bookbinding in all its varieties. Wordsworth [g] has given several details of the work they executed.

HONOURABLE ROGER NORTH.

This distinguished man of his time was, in his younger days, passionately fond of the art bibliopegistic, and pursued it with creditable success. His relative, in his biography, thus speaks of this peculiarity of his character :—

" The young gentleman took a fancy to the binding of books, and having procured a stitching-board, press, and cutter, fell to work, and bound up books of account for himself, and divers for his friends, in a very decent manner."[h]

WILLIAM HUTTON,

who, from being a stocking-weaver, in the most abject state of poverty, raised himself to affluence, and the respect and regard of the learned and wealthy, was originally an amateur bookbinder. To this circumstance the success of his career may, without cavil, be principally attributed. It is curious to trace his progress, as he has recounted in his Life. He was fond of books and music, and, in 1746, he says, " an inclination for books began to expand, but here,

g Eccl. Biography, v. 172—178, 216, 220, 257.——h North's Life of Sir Dudley North.

as in music and dress, money was wanting. The first articles of purchase were three volumes of the Gentleman's Magazine, 1742, 3, and 4. As I could not afford to pay for binding, I fastened them together in a most cobbling style. These afforded me a treat.

" I could only raise books of small value, and these in worn-out bindings. I learnt to patch, procuring paste, varnish, &c., and brought them into tolerable order, erected shelves, and arranged them in the best manner I was able.

" If I purchased shabby books, it is no wonder that I dealt with a shabby bookseller, who kept his working apparatus in his shop. It is no wonder, too, if by repeated visits I became acquainted with this shabby bookseller, and often saw him at work; but it is a wonder, and a fact, that I never saw him perform one act but I could perform it myself; so strong was the desire to attain the art.

" I made no secret of my progress, and the bookseller rather encouraged me, and that for two reasons : I bought such rubbish as nobody else would; and he had often an opportunity of selling me a cast-off tool for a shilling, not worth a penny. As I was below every degree of opposition, a rivalship was out of the question.

" The first book I bound was a very small one—Shakspeare's Venus and Adonis. I showed it to the bookseller. He seemed surprised. I could see jealousy in his eye. However, he recovered in a

moment, and observed, that though he had sold me
the books and tools *remarkably cheap*, he could not
think of giving so much for them again. He had no
doubt but I should break.

" He offered me a worn-down press for two shillings, which no man could use, and which was laid
by for the fire. I considered the nature of its construction, bought it, and paid the two shillings. I
then asked him to favour me with a hammer and a
pin, which he brought with half a conquering smile
and half a sneer. I drove out the garter pin, which,
being galled, prevented the press from working, and
turned another square, which perfectly cured the
press. He said in anger, ' If I had known, you
should not have had it! This proved for forty-two
years my best binding press.' " [i]

From an amateur, Hutton soon became a professed
bookbinder: for we find him, in 1748, thus express
himself :—" Every soul who knew me scoffed at the
idea of my turning bookbinder, except my sister,
who encouraged and aided me, otherwise I must
have sunk under it. I hated stocking-making, but not
bookbinding. I still pursued the two trades. Hurt
to see my three vols of Magazines in so degraded a
state, I took them to pieces, and clothed them in a
superior dress." And again in 1749. " A bookbinder,
fostered by the stocking frame, was such a novelty, that
many people gave me a book to bind. Hitherto I had

[i] Hutton's Life, 130—2.

only used the wretched tools, and the materials for binding, which my bookseller chose to sell me ; but I found there were many things wanting, which were only to be had in London ; besides, I wished to fix a correspondence for what I wanted, without purchasing at second hand. There was a necessity to take this journey; but an obstacle arose,—I had no money."

This journey took him nine days, walking to London and back again, and of his extraordinary economy, his expenses during that time are a proof, having expended no more than eight shillings and fourpence. He says, " I only wanted three alphabets, a set of figures, and some ornamental tools for gilding books ; with leather and boards for binding." He fixed at Southwell, in Nottinghamshire, " took a shop at the rate of twenty shillings a year, sent a few boards for shelves, a few tools, and about two cwt. of trash, and became the most eminent bookseller in the place."[k] His subsequent life is well known.

The last name in our biographical notices, is one now become celebrated as of the most distinguished chemist of the day, viz.

MICHAEL FARADAY.

This eminent person was the son of a humble blacksmith, who apprenticed him to a small book-

[k] Hutton's Life, 137, 138, 145.

binder in Blandford Street, when only nine years of age, and in which occupation he continued till he. was twenty-two. The circumstances that occasioned his exchanging the work-room of the binder for the laboratory of the chemist, have been thus forcibly related. Ned Magrath, now secretary to the Athenæum, happening five and twenty years ago to enter the shop of Ribeau, observed one of the bucks of the paper bonnet zealously studying a book he ought to have been binding. He approached—it was a volume of the old *Britannica*, open at ELECTRICITY. He entered into talk with the greasy journeyman, and was astonished to find in him a self-taught chemist of no slender pretensions. He presented him with a set of tickets for Davy's lectures at the Royal Institution; and daily thereafter might the nondescript be seen perched, pen in hand, and his eyes starting out of his head, just over the clock opposite the chair. At last the course terminated; but Faraday's spirit had received a new impulse, which nothing but dire necessity could have restrained; and from that he was saved by the promptitude with which, on his forwarding a modest outline of his history, with the notes he had made of these lectures, to Davy, that great and good man rushed to the rescue of kindred genius. Sir Humphrey immediately appointed him an assistant in the laboratory; and. after two or three years had passed, he found Faraday qualified to act as his secretary.[1]

Frazer's Mag, xiii. 224.

His career has been successful, and he now stands at the head of his profession. He ranks as one of the first lecturers of the day, and has published several works highly and deservedly popular.

CONCLUSION.

Our endeavours to illustrate the rise and progress of the art of writing and composing books, and the successive improvements in bookbinding, are now brought to a termination. The simple records of the earliest people; the rolls of the Greeks and Romans; the massy and costly books of the monasteries and churches; the elaborately ornamented volumes of a later period,

> " Firmly clasp'd in oak, and velvet bound ;"

and the highly-finished works of modern days; with other incidental matter, have been enlarged upon. With what degree of success, it is for others now to arbitrate. We close, therefore, our account with the description of the Art in the well-known Poem, " The Press," by Mr. M'Creery.

> " Embodied thought enjoys a splendid rest
> On guardian shelves, in emblem costume drest;
> Like gems that sparkle in the parent mine,
> Through crystal mediums the rich coverings shine ;
> Morocco flames in scarlet, blue, and green,
> Impress'd with burnish'd gold, of dazzling sheen;
> Arms deep emboss'd the owner's state declare,
> Test of their worth—their age—and his kind care ;

Embalm'd in russia stands a valued pile,
That time impairs not, nor foul worms defile ;
Russia, exhaling from its scented pores
Its saving power to these thrice-valued stores.
In order fair arranged the volumes stand,
Gay with the skill of many a modern hand ;
At the expense of sinew and of bone,
The fine papyrian leaves are firm as stone :
Here all is square as by masonic rule,
And bright the impression of the burnished tool.
On some the tawny calf a coat bestows,
Where flowers and fillets beauteous forms compose ;
Others in pride the virgin vellum wear,
Beaded with gold—as breast of Venus fair ;
On either end the silken head-bands twine,
Wrought by some maid with skilful fingers fine—
The yielding back falls loose, the hinges play,
And the rich page lies open to the day.
Where science traces the unerring line,
In brilliant tints the forms of beauty shine ;
These, in our works, as in a casket laid,
Increase the splendour by their powerful aid."

THE FRONTISPIECE.

The engraved frontispiece is designed to embody various specimens of ancient art. The one on the stand, to the left, is a representation of the binding of an Aldine Cicero of the sixteenth century, now in King's library, Cambridge. By the side of it, on the right, is shown the back and side of the "Manual of Prayers," belonging to queen Elizabeth, described at page 83. Below, on the left, is a sketch of the binding of the "Acta Synodi Dort," in the British Museum, referred to at the seventy-ninth page; and to the right a specimen of the baass-bound volumes of the fifteenth century, from Lincoln cathedral.

INDEX.

FINIS.

London: G. H. Davidson, Printer, Tudor Street, Blackfriars' Bridge.

For EU product safety concerns, contact us at Calle de José Abascal, 56–1°,
28003 Madrid, Spain or eugpsr@cambridge.org.

www.ingramcontent.com/pod-product-compliance
Ingram Content Group UK Ltd.
Pitfield, Milton Keynes, MK11 3LW, UK
UKHW010338140625
459647UK00010B/690